THE QUESTION OF
JEAN-JACQUES ROUSSEAU

ERNST CASSIRER

The Question of
Jean-Jacques Rousseau

TRANSLATED AND EDITED WITH AN
INTRODUCTION AND ADDITIONAL NOTES

by PETER GAY

Indiana University Press

BLOOMINGTON & LONDON

PREFACE TO MIDLAND BOOK EDITION

THE RECENT LITERATURE on Rousseau has set itself a demanding task: to write biographical studies which leave external biography behind, and intellectual history which moves from ideas to existence. These books are steps toward, but not yet realizations of, that most desirable and most elusive of goals: a complete biography of Rousseau. In his study of Rousseau's "philosophy of existence," Pierre Burgelin has tried to penetrate his masks, his moods, his inconsistencies to discover the unity of his thought;[1] while, from a completely different direction, Jean Guéhenno has used all the available material—the autobiographical works, the correspondence, and the writings—to reconstruct Rousseau's work from the inside, to discover what it was like to *be* Rousseau at any given moment by surrendering all the advantages of hindsight, and to establish the intimate relevance of life to work.[2] Guéhenno's recreation is a much-needed corrective to the deceptive *Confessions,* an illuminating and moving first essay in that complete biography. With similarly deliberate naïveté, Jean Starobinski has tried to sort out Rousseau's central concerns, his obsessive images and driving urges: he has written a book that follows a chronological order

[1] Pierre Burgelin, *La philosophie de l'existence de J.-J. Rousseau* (Paris, 1952).

[2] Jean Guéhenno, *Jean-Jacques* (Paris, 1948-1952), 3 vols. Much the best recent biography in English is F. C. Green, *Jean-Jacques Rousseau: A Critical Study of His Life and Writings* (Cambridge, England, 1955), sensitive on his literary personality but weak on Rousseau's politics.

without being a biography, and a psychological analysis that is not content with mere *analyse intérieure*. To Starobinski, the inner drama of Rousseau is the conflict of his desire for "transparency"—for clarity and honesty—with the "obstacle"—the frustrations imposed by inner turmoil and external difficulties.[3]

While these books have passed beyond Cassirer, they have used the methods or confirmed the stature of Cassirer's essay. Indeed, Burgelin explicitly echoes Cassirer's methodological principle that "Rousseau's fundamental thought, although it had its immediate origin in his nature and individuality, was neither circumscribed by nor bound to that individual personality; that in its maturity and perfection this thought puts before us an objective formulation of questions; and that this formulation is valid not for him or his era alone but contains, in full sharpness and definiteness, an inner, strictly objective necessity."[4] With this principle, worked out in these recent books, we can hope that the expectation of a complete biography of Rousseau may soon be realized, a work that will do even-handed justice to all the dimensions of his life, his thought, his times, and his importance. When that biography is written, it will be psychological analysis and literary criticism, political theory and social history, educational program and philosophical speculation. And when it is written, it is safe to predict that its author will have been significantly influenced by Ernst Cassirer's *Question of Jean Jacques Rousseau*.

P. G.

---

3 Jean Starobinski, *Jean-Jacques Rousseau: La transparence et l'obstacle* (Paris, 1957). There is a subtle essay on all aspects of Rousseau's work, Bernard Groethuysen's *J.-J. Rousseau* (Paris, 1949), which was published posthumously and represented, with excessive modesty, as a series of notes. It is in fact a rich work, viewing Rousseau as perpetually in opposition to reigning values ready, at the same time, to concede virtue to his opponents. To Groethuysen, Rousseau's philosophy is a philosophy of choice.

4 Burgelin, *op. cit.*, 12-13; see below, p. 40.

CONTENTS

INTRODUCTION

*Il faut étudier la société par les hommes,
et les hommes par la société: ceux qui
voudront traiter séparément la politique
et la morale n'entendront jamais rien à
aucune des deux.*

JEAN-JACQUES ROUSSEAU, Emile

Fᴏʀ ᴀʟᴍᴏsᴛ ᴛᴡᴏ ᴄᴇɴᴛᴜʀɪᴇs the philosophy of Rousseau
has perplexed its interpreters. Among the many critics who have
tried to deal with it, one of the greatest—but for a long time one
of the most neglected—was Jean-Jacques Rousseau himself. In his
Confessions he emphasized that his writings, taken as a whole, revealed a consistent and coherent philosophy: "All that is daring in
the *Contrat social* had previously appeared in the *Discours sur
l'inégalité;* all that is daring in *Emile* had previously appeared in
Julie." [1] The discrepancies that the reader might find in them were,
he said, purely superficial.[2] He reiterated this conviction, which
must have been of great importance to him, as he came to reflect
on his work once more near the end of his life: "One great principle," he maintained, was evident in all his books.[3]

Only a handful of Rousseau's interpreters were to take this self-
estimate seriously. Instead, the majority of his critics searched for,
and pretended to find, the "essence of Rousseau" in one or the

[1] *Confessions,* Livre ɪx (*Œuvres complètes,* Hachette ed., [Paris, 1871–77],
VIII, 290–91). Cf. also *ibid.,* Livre xɪɪ (Hachette ed., IX, 69, 70).

[2] *Ibid.,* Livre ɪx (Hachette ed., VIII, 277n), where he attributes the "harsh
tone and gloomy air" of the *Discours sur l'inégalité* to Diderot's influence.

[3] *Rousseau juge de Jean-Jacques,* Troisième Dialogue (Hachette ed., IX, 287).

other of his major works or in some of his scintillating epigrams.[4] Worse, a number of Rousseau scholars inferred the supposed confusion or self-contradictory character of his work from the undeniable fact that his writings served as the inspiration for widely divergent movements, overlooking the notorious tendency of disciples to distort the philosophy of their master by selecting only what they need. Many thinkers have suffered at the hands of commentators, but few have had to endure as much as Rousseau. Conflicting claims, pronounced with equal certitude, have obscured that integrity of his thought on which he had insisted so often.

Ernst Cassirer's essay, "Das Problem Jean Jacques Rousseau," accepts Rousseau's contention and attempts to reveal the meaning of his thought by providing an understanding of his work as a whole. The magnitude of Cassirer's achievement can best be grasped if we briefly survey the Rousseau interpretations which his essay was designed to refute.

II

The influence of Rousseau's doctrines has been immense— they left their mark on the most diverse spirits and movements. Burke execrated Rousseau as the very embodiment of the Age of Reason. De Maistre and Bonald condemned him as the advocate of an irresponsible individualism and as the philosopher of ruinous disorder. Later critics, such as Sir Henry Maine, attacked him for establishing a "collective despot" and for reintroducing, in the *Contrat social,* "the old divine right of kings in a new dress." [5]

---

[4] Gustave Lanson, himself a leading Rousseau interpreter, propounded some sensible canons of interpretation: "To weigh seriously the meaning and import of the texts, and to consider the spirit more than the letter. . . . Not to substitute for [the author's] thought the consequences which have been deduced from it. . . . To assign to his ideas their proper significance." "L'Unité de la pensée de Jean-Jacques Rousseau," *Annales de la Société Jean-Jacques Rousseau,* VIII (1912), 6.

[5] *Popular Government* (New York: Holt, 1886), pp. 157, 160.

4

Rousseau's disciples contradicted each other as vigorously as his opponents did. The Jacobins established the Reign of Terror in his name; the German romantics hailed him as a liberator; Schiller pictured him as a martyr to wisdom:

> Sokrates ging unter durch Sophisten,
> Rousseau leidet, Rousseau fällt durch Christen,
> Rousseau—der aus Christen Menschen wirbt.[6]

Edmund Burke, Rousseau's most formidable antagonist in the eighteenth century, was surely right when he said, "I believe, that, were Rousseau alive, and in one of his lucid intervals, he would be shocked at the practical frenzy of his scholars. . . ."[7]

The conflict of interpretations by no means diminished after Rousseau had ceased to be a symbol in the political struggle. Long after the smoke of revolution and reaction had cleared away, Rousseau was still praised or condemned for the widest variety of reasons. Cassirer's essay shows that these disagreements were not confined to Rousseau's political theory. Rousseau was called rationalist and irrationalist by turns; his economics was described as socialist or as founded on the sanctity of private property; his religion was seen as Deist, Catholic, or Protestant; his moral teachings were alternately held to be Puritanical or too emotional and relaxed.

However, since most of his commentators have treated Rousseau as a political theorist, or have judged his thought in the light of his political philosophy, political categories will prove most useful in an analysis of the literature. Rousseau, it has been said, is an

---

[6] Schiller, "Rousseau":

> As Socrates by sophists was brought low,
> So Christians tortured, Christians felled Rousseau—
> Rousseau, who called on Christians to be men.

For a more detailed discussion of Rousseau's influence, see Alfred Cobban, *Rousseau and the Modern State* (London: Allen and Unwin, 1934), Chap. ii.

[7] *Reflections on the Revolution in France*, in *Orations and Essays* (New York: Appleton, 1900), p. 529.

individualist—a collectivist—a writer whose doctrines are deeply self-contradictory—a man who shifted in mid-career from individualism to collectivism.

In the first decades after Rousseau's death, both the counterrevolutionaries, such as De Maistre (to whom Rousseau was the incarnation of political impiety), and the radicals, such as the representatives of *Sturm und Drang* (who acclaimed him as the prophet of the coming age of freedom), considered Rousseau the exemplar of individualism. Hölderlin, who called him a demigod, translated Rousseau's purported defiance of the chains of law into extravagant verse.[8]

This conception of Rousseau as an individualist arose before the opposite point of view became popular, and it has never gone wholly out of fashion.[9] Several notable French commentators defended it skillfully. Thus Emile Faguet argued that "all of Rousseau can be found in the *Discours sur l'inégalité.* That is a commonplace . . . but I believe it to be true."[10] And this "novel of humanity," as Faguet calls it, has one central theme: man is good and becomes evil by embracing society. Faguet felt constrained to admit that the *Contrat social* is "antiliberal" and that Rousseau's political thought contains "not an atom of liberty or security."[11] But he explains his difficulty away: the *Contrat social* "seems an

[8] See esp. Hölderlin's "Hymne an die Freiheit," "Hymne an die Menschheit," "Rousseau," and "Der Rhein." In the last-named poem Rousseau's message to man is a revelation which the demigod transmits to humanity and which Hölderlin characteristically sees as *gesetzlos*—lawless.

[9] Cf. Cobban, *Rousseau and the Modern State*, pp. 33–43. When C. E. Vaughan published his celebrated edition of the *Political Writings of Jean Jacques Rousseau* (2 vols.; Cambridge: Cambridge University Press, 1915), he said in the Introduction (p. 1): "The work of Rousseau is little known in this country and less understood. The title of the *Contrat social* is familiar. But to most men it suggests an extreme form of individualism."

[10] *Dix-huitième siècle*, 43d ed. (Paris: Société française d'imprimerie et de librairie, n. d.), p. 345.

[11] *Ibid.*, pp. 401, 403.

6

isolated part of Rousseau's work" and "contradicts his general ideas." [12] Rousseau's political theory is but an aberration. On the other hand, the individualist conception of the *Discours sur l'inégalité*, "the antisocial idea," [13] is fundamental —it runs through nearly all his writings and appears with particular impressiveness in *Emile*.[14]

A quarter of a century later, Henri Sée arrived at a similar conclusion by a different logical path. "The *Discours sur l'inégalité*," he wrote in full agreement with Faguet, "is inspired by an individualist, indeed almost anarchist, conception. But," and at this point he departs from Faguet, "in the *Contrat social* Rousseau remains an individualist, despite appearances to the contrary." [15] Rousseau's political theory revolves around the attempt to "assure the individual the full development of his liberty," [16] and, Sée concludes, "Rousseau appears to us . . . as an individualist and a liberal. It is not true that he wants to give the state an absolute and aggressive authority." [17]

Probably the most significant source for the opposite contention, that Rousseau is a collectivist, is Taine's *Ancien Régime*. It was Taine's belief that the French Revolution—in which "brutal force placed itself at the disposal of radical dogma, and . . . radical dogma placed itself at the disposal of brutal force," [18]—had largely been the work of intellectuals whose knowledge of the world of men was slight. Consequently, these intellectuals had indulged without restraint in abstract theorizing which eventually infected the French mind with the sickness of revolutionary ideas.[19] View-

---

[12] *Ibid.*, p. 400.   [13] *Ibid.*, p. 399.   [14] *Ibid.*, pp. 360–77, 400.

[15] *L'Evolution de la pensée politique en France au XVIIIe siècle* (Paris: Marcel Giard, 1925), p. 146.

[16] *Ibid.*   [17] *Ibid.*, p. 161.

[18] *Les Origines de la France contemporaine*, Vol. I: *L'Ancien Régime* (Paris: Hachette, 1896), p. 521. This volume first appeared in 1876.

[19] For a brief, perceptive criticism of Taine, see Edmund Wilson, *To the Finland Station* (New York: Doubleday, 1953), pp. 44–54, and Henri Peyre, "The In-

ing Rousseau as the prototype of these pernicious philosophers, Taine gave a new twist to Rousseau criticism. Rousseau's political theory, he argued, had been designed as the supreme assault on law and the state and had resulted, paradoxically but inevitably, in tyranny: "The doctrine of popular sovereignty, interpreted by the masses, will produce perfect anarchy until the moment when, interpreted by the rulers, it will produce perfect despotism." [20] Rousseau's state, as he put it in an epigram to which Cassirer refers, is a "layman's monastery," and "in this democratic monastery which Rousseau establishes on the model of Sparta and Rome, the individual is nothing and the state everything." [21]

This and similar views have now become predominant in the literature.[22] We can hear echoes of it in Karl Popper's description of Rousseau's thought as "romantic collectivism" [23] and in Sir Ernest Barker's, "In effect, and in the last resort, Rousseau is a totalitarian. . . . Imagine Rousseau a perfect democrat: his perfect democracy is still a multiple autocracy." [24] Many, although certainly not all, present-day readers of Rousseau, remembering the supremacy of the general will, the forcing men to be free, the civil religion, and forgetting the rest of his writings, will agree with Taine and Barker. The fashion in fact is to consider Rousseau a totalitarian—a "democratic totalitarian" perhaps, but a totalitarian nevertheless.

---

fluence of Eighteenth Century Ideas on the French Revolution," in *The Making of Modern Europe,* ed. by Herman Ausubel (New York: Dryden, 1951), I, 470–72. Taine's critique of Rousseau can be traced to De Maistre and Bonald.

[20] Taine, *L'Ancien Régime,* p. 319.

[21] *Ibid.,* pp. 323, 321.

[22] Cobban says that "practically all the modern literary criticism of Rousseau is derived" from Taine. *Rousseau and the Modern State,* p. 40.

[23] K. R. Popper, *The Open Society and its Enemies* (London: Routledge, 1945), II, 50.

[24] Introduction to *The Social Contract* (New York: Oxford University Press, 1948), p. xxxviii.

8

III

These two irreconcilable interpretations of Rousseau's thought have been supplemented by two other views: it has been argued that his doctrines are confused and rent by internal contradictions, or that they shifted from one extreme to the other as they were developed and elaborated. Faguet saves his interpretation of Rousseau as an individualist by writing off what he assumed to be the collectivist implications of the *Contrat social*. Barker, who after some hesitation ranks Rousseau among the collectivists, professes to be unable to find a real core in his thought: "You can find your own dogmas in Rousseau, whether you belong to the Left (and especially to the left of the Left) or whether you belong to the Right (and especially to the right of the Right.)" [25]

Much earlier, John Morley had made this point even more emphatically. He accused Rousseau of neglecting the only sources of evidence—history and experience—on which a sound social theory could be based. He derided what he called Rousseau's "narrow, symmetrical, impatient humor" and the "desperate absurdity of the assumptions of the Social Contract." [26] Following Burke, he described Rousseau as the "typical schoolman" who "assumes that analysis of terms is the right way of acquiring new knowledge about things" and who "mistakes the multiplication of propositions for the discovery of fresh truth." [27] "Many pages of the Social Contract," Morley concluded, "are mere logical deductions from verbal definitions, which the slightest attempt to

[25] *Ibid.*, p. xxxix.

[26] Morley, *Rousseau* (London: Chapman and Hall, 1873), II, 126, 134.

[27] *Ibid.*, II, 135. Morley would not even grant that Rousseau practiced the scholastic method skillfully: "Rousseau was always apt to think in a slipshod manner." *Ibid.*, I, 192.

confront with actual fact would have shown to be not only value-less, but wholly meaningless. . . ." [28]

This conception of the "confused" Rousseau has also gained wide currency, although the critics who espouse it have been unable to make up their minds whether Rousseau's doctrine is worthless because of the deductive and abstract logic from which it springs or whether, as Irving Babbitt was to argue, Rousseau was betrayed by lack of method and by romantic emotionalism.

This attitude toward Rousseau's thought is partly redeemed by the work of C. E. Vaughan, a scholar to whom all who work the rich mine of Rousseau's political theory owe a great debt. In 1915, after many years of collecting and collating all the available manuscripts, Vaughan published the definitive texts of Rousseau's political writings and prefaced them with a substantial introduction. His solid two-volume work has been very influential—and rightfully so. Like Cassirer after him, Vaughan sees Rousseau's thought as a problem demanding solution rather than a dogma requiring exposition: "Strike out the *Discours sur l'inégalité* with the first few pages of the *Contrat social,* and the 'individualism' of Rousseau will be seen to be nothing better than a myth." [29] While the *Discours sur l'inégalité* "suggested . . . if it did not explicitly proclaim, a more extreme form of individualism than any previous writer had ventured to set forth," [30] the compact with which the *Contrat social* begins "forms the porch to a collectivism as absolute as the mind of man has ever conceived." [31] Nor will it be easy to reconcile these two strands that lie side by side in Rousseau's political thought: "When all is said, the two rival elements, the individual and the community, are left not so much reconciled, as in ill-veiled hostility, to each other." [32]

Vaughan believes that the chief task of Rousseau interpretation

[28] *Ibid.,* II, 135. [29] *The Political Writings of Jean Jacques Rousseau,* I, 2.
[30] *Ibid.,* I, 119. [31] *Ibid.,* I, 39. [32] *Ibid.,* I, 5.

10

is to account for or to solve this conflict, for which he himself offers three separate explanations. First, he argues that the early Discourses were primarily moral in character, pointing to existing vices by means of extreme statement.[33] This is a prescient hint which anticipates the attempts of such critics as Cassirer and Charles W. Hendel to overcome the supposed contradictions in Rousseau's thought by viewing Rousseau as fundamentally a moralist. Secondly, Vaughan draws attention to the conflict between abstract and concrete thought in Rousseau. The former, derived largely from Locke and Plato, pushes him into extreme and unqualified statements; the latter, inherited from Montesquieu, leads him to the conviction that life is never clear-cut and that principles are modified by circumstances. Vaughan finds a growing concern with concreteness in Rousseau's work, a concern that gains the upper hand in the later chapters of the *Contrat social* and becomes fully dominant in his last political writings, particularly in the *Lettres écrites de la montagne* and the *Gouvernement de Pologne*.[34]

Vaughan's third explanation, however, is far more important: Rousseau's intellectual labors must be understood as a journey of growth from individualism to collectivism.

The political work of Rousseau, when taken as a whole, presents an unbroken movement from one position almost to its opposite. He starts as the prophet of freedom, in the most abstract sense conceivable. His ideal, in the second *Discourse*, is a state of things in which each individual is absolutely independent of the rest. . . . Save for those opening sentences, the *Contrat social* represents a very different—and

[33] *Ibid.*, I, 7, 14.

[34] *Ibid.*, I, 77–78. This explanation is not satisfactory. It is true that Rousseau does not clearly distinguish between abstract universal principles and concrete statements, and this helps to account for his tendency to take back by means of qualification what he establishes with a sweeping generalization: but this tendency can be found in all his work and is not significant enough to account for the supposed conflict.

assuredly a less abstract, as well as a less individualist—idea. Here freedom is no longer conceived as the independence of the individual. It is rather to be sought in his total surrender to the service of the State. . . .

Silent though it is, the change of tone and temper is complete. . . . The abstract individualism of the second *Discourse,* the abstract collectivism of the *Contrat social,* are alike forgotten [in the last political writings]. . . . The long journey is at last ended. And Rousseau now stands at the opposite point of the compass from that at which he started.[35]

The undeniable merits of Vaughan's edition must not blind us to its deficiencies. The very defects which Vaughan professes to find in Rousseau—the tendencies to overstatement and vacillation—are curiously present in his own work, and he divines the unity of Rousseau's thought only in occasional glimpses.[36] Moreover, by confining his edition to Rousseau's *political* writings, Vaughan emphasizes one facet of Rousseau's thought at the expense of the rest and makes an understanding of Rousseau's meaning impossible. Of course, Rousseau was a political theorist, and a great one. But this is all the more reason for making a careful study of *Emile,* the *Nouvelle Héloïse,* and the *Confessions*— books that illuminate and give proper balance to Rousseau's

[35] *Ibid.,* I, 80–81. This interpretation, although it has some superficial resemblance to Taine's "from absolute freedom to absolute despotism," is yet to be distinguished from it. Vaughan sees Rousseau's change as a temporal process, Taine sees it as a logical development inherent in Rousseau's doctrines. Indeed, although Vaughan calls Rousseau the "most powerful assailant" of individualism (*ibid.,* I, 1), he is far from following Taine in portraying him as a proponent of despotism.

[36] For example, Vaughan writes: "If Rousseau exalts the State, and exalts it unduly, at the expense of the individual, it must not be forgotten of what nature is the State that he has in mind." *Ibid.,* I, 112. E. H. Wright and Cassirer later insisted that one important clue to the unity of Rousseau's thought lay in the special meaning which he gave the word "natural." They argued that while Rousseau indeed exalted the state he did so only with the understanding that it was a very special kind of state—a state that did not yet exist—which would not abuse its sovereignty. Vaughan never developed this idea beyond a hint.

political philosophy. Vaughan's edition shows unwittingly that the critic who wants to understand Rousseau must transcend political categories and consider his work as a whole.

IV

The blame for the multiplicity of opinions in the Rousseau literature cannot be placed solely on his interpreters. If Cassirer is right in believing that Rousseau was, in fact, neither confused nor inconsistent, we may conclude that Rousseau, like Nietzsche after him, invited misunderstanding. Why?

David Hume wrote about Rousseau in 1766: "Really his Writings are so full of Extravagance, that I cannot believe their Eloquence alone will be able to support them." [37] But it was Rousseau's eloquence rather than his extravagance that created difficulties for the commentators. Rousseau was, unhappily, the coiner of happy phrases. Read in context, they were usually elucidated by the argument in which they were embedded. Taken out of context, their rhetorical power obscured the fact that they were only elliptical pronouncements. Used as slogans, they twisted or destroyed his meaning.

Three examples from Rousseau's writings will give us the full flavor of what Henri Peyre, following Alfred Fouillée, has called *idées-forces*.[38] "L'homme qui médite est un animal dépravé" [39] has been quoted again and again as proof that Rousseau despised thought and rationality. "L'homme est né libre, et partout il est dans les fers" [40] has been mistaken for the first sentence of a paean to extreme individualism; no wonder that readers of the

[37] J. Y. T. Greig, ed. *The Letters of David Hume* (Oxford: Clarendon Press, 1932), II, 103.

[38] "The Influence of Eighteenth Century Ideas on the French Revolution," in *The Making of Modern Europe*, I, 484.

[39] *Discours sur l'inégalité*, Première Partie (Hachette ed., I, 87).

[40] *Contrat social*, opening sentence of Chap. i.

Contrat social who took this statement literally were disappointed in the rest of the treatise. "Commençons donc par écarter tous les faits, car ils ne touchent point à la question" [41] has been offered as conclusive demonstration of Rousseau's lack of interest in empirical evidence and of his preference for abstract propositions spun out in indifference to, or even defiance of, the truth.

A careful and sympathetic reading of his full work would remove the obstacles which such sentences introduce, but Rousseau rarely found such readers. "In lapidary inscriptions a man is not upon oath," Samuel Johnson once said about epitaphs; readers of Rousseau should keep a similar caution in mind. Rousseau himself realized that his intensely personal style might offer difficulties to his readers, and what he wrote to Madame d'Epinay about his use of language in correspondence may be applied with equal force to the writings he intended for publication: "Learn my vocabulary better, my good friend, if you would have us understand each other. Believe me, my terms rarely have the common meaning; it is always my heart that converses with you, and perhaps you will learn some day that it speaks not as others do." [42]

It was not only Rousseau's style that led many of his interpreters astray. Another source of misconceptions was the fascination which his life exercised on their imaginations and critical faculties. "The self-torturing sophist, wild Rousseau," Byron called him,

> The apostle of affliction, he who threw
> Enchantment over passion, and from woe
> Wrung overwhelming eloquence. . . . [43]

Many of Rousseau's commentators gave in to the temptation of reducing the philosophy of the "apostle of affliction" to a mere

[41] *Discours sur l'inégalité*, Première Partie (Hachette ed., I, 83).

[42] March 1756. Théophile Dufour, ed., *Correspondance générale de J.-J. Rousseau* (Paris: Colin, 1924–34), II, 266. Cf. below, pp. 127–28.

[43] *Childe Harold's Pilgrimage*, Canto the Third, stanza LXXVII.

reflection of his experiences—or rather, to a reflection of the twisted interpretations which he gave to these experiences. Cassirer had this kind of criticism in mind when he wrote, "There are familiar writings in the Rousseau literature which give us in place of the work almost the man alone, and which describe him only in his dissensions and divisions, in his inner contradictions. The history of ideas threatens here to disappear into biography, and this in turn appears as a pure case history." [44]

To be sure, the genetic explanation, the biographic approach, will give insight into the motives of a writer and aid inquiry into the personal or social origin of his doctrines. It will help to explain why an author writes a certain book, and why he holds certain beliefs—but the objective validity of his doctrines is unaffected by the personal history of their creator. The fact that Rousseau confesses to abandoning his five natural children at a foundling home does not affect the merits of the educational plan in *Emile*. His paranoid quarrels with the Encyclopedists may illuminate his motives for publishing the *Contrat social* but they do not invalidate (or improve) the logic of his political theory. These canons of interpretation have been disregarded by many of Rousseau's critics. F. J. C. Hearnshaw writes, for example: "So intimately . . . were Rousseau's writings associated with his life that it is impossible to comprehend them without a detailed knowledge of his curious and remarkable career." [45] Fortified by this statement, he divides Rousseau's life into five periods: the undisciplined boy, the supertramp, the would-be man of the world, the inspired maniac, the hunted fugitive.[46] Hearnshaw, thus spared the

[44] *Rousseau, Kant, Goethe* (Princeton: Princeton University Press, 1947), p. 58. In a footnote to this passage Cassirer mentions Irving Babbitt as one of the offenders.

[45] "Rousseau," in F. J. C. Hearnshaw, ed., *The Social and Political Ideas of some Great French Thinkers of the Age of Reason* (London: Harrap, 1930), p. 172.

[46] *Ibid.*, pp. 173, 175, 176, 178, 183. See also the lurid character sketch in Taine, *L'Ancien Régime*, p. 289.

necessity of seriously grappling with Rousseau's meaning, can sum up one of the greatest of all political theorists with these words: "He was an unsystematic thinker, untrained in formal logic. He was an omnivorous reader with undeveloped powers of assimilation. He was an emotional enthusiast who spoke without due reflection. He was an irresponsible writer with a fatal gift for epigram." [47]

This general line of interpretation was pursued to its extreme by Irving Babbitt. His *Rousseau and Romanticism,* which is filled with ill-tempered denunciations of Rousseau, displays to the point of caricature the crippling weaknesses of a preoccupation with biography. Babbitt dismisses Rousseau's trenchant critique of eighteenth-century society in these words: "Rousseau's spite against eighteenth-century Paris was largely due to the fact that he had not acquired young enough the habits that would have made it possible for him to conform to its conventions." He demolishes Rousseau's solution of the theodicy problem by saying, "The faith in one's natural goodness is a constant encouragement to evade moral responsibility." He disdainfully contrasts Rousseau's statements on love, which remind him "of the cult of the medieval knight for his lady," with his practice: "So much for the ideal; the real was Thérèse Levasseur." [48]

It is plain that a critic who makes such ill use of the biographical method is likely to misrepresent a thinker whose life story he despises. Babbitt succeeds in misunderstanding Rousseau's doctrines with astonishing consistency: "Rousseau . . . look[s] upon every constraint whether from within or from without as incompatible with liberty." "His programme amounts in practice to the indulgence of infinite indeterminate desire." "One may learn

[47] Hearnshaw, "Rousseau," pp. 185–86.

[48] *Rousseau and Romanticism* (Boston: Houghton, Mifflin, 1919), pp. 174, 155, 221, 220.

from Rousseau the art of sinking to the region of instinct that is below the rational level instead of struggling forward to the region of insight that is above it." [49]

V

Around the turn of this century a small band of scholars began to go back to Rousseau's work in its entirety and to extract from it the basic unity of his thought. These critics had not lost interest in the question of Rousseau's individualism or collectivism, but such political categories no longer held a central place in their attention. Instead, they sought to widen the horizon of interpretation. They did not deny the paradoxical character of many of Rousseau's pronouncements, but they agreed with Rousseau that these paradoxes do not impair his fundamental consistency. The most notable contributions to this search for Rousseau's "one great principle" were made by Gustave Lanson, E. H. Wright, and, in 1932, by Ernst Cassirer.[50]

Lanson, author of a celebrated history of French literature, describes Rousseau as an individualist.[51] But, in full agreement with E. H. Wright, he does not regard this as the key to the unity of Rousseau's thought. Wright's penetrating comment on the *Contrat social,* that "the book is meant for neither individualist nor absolutist," [52] could serve as the motto for both Wright's and Lanson's estimates of Rousseau's entire work. What is central to Lanson's view is Rousseau's own statement of his "great principle," enunciated in the first sentence of *Emile,* implied through all

[49] *Ibid.,* pp. 377–78, 79, 154.

[50] Cassirer mentions other writers who have argued for the unity of Rousseau's thought. Cf. below, p. 53. We should add Harald Höffding, *Rousseau und seine Philosophie* (Stuttgart: Frommann, 1897), and G. D. H. Cole's Introduction to *The Social Contract and Discourses* (London: Dent, 1913).

[51] *Histoire de la littérature française,* 8th ed. (Paris: Hachette, 1903), p. 775.

[52] E. H. Wright, *The Meaning of Rousseau* (London: Oxford University Press, 1929), p. 103.

his work, and again expressed in *Rousseau juge de Jean-Jacques:* "Que la nature a fait l'homme heureux et bon, mais que la société le déprave et le rend misérable." [53] This principle, Lanson holds, is the key to Rousseau's philosophy: the essential vice of society, the *Discours sur l'inégalité* tells us, is an inequality that is not ordained by nature—the inequality created by wealth and poverty.[54] The *Contrat social* exemplifies this principle in conjunction with another on which Rousseau always insisted: "La nature humaine ne rétrograde pas." [55] The natural man cannot escape society but must recreate it to recreate himself. The educational program of *Emile* follows logically: it outlines the growth of the "natural man . . . with all the advantages and without any of the vices of the civilized man." [56] The *Nouvelle Héloïse* furnishes further details on the same theme: it establishes the moral values of personal relations without which neither the individual nor society can become truly good. Finally, Rousseau's system includes God in its scheme in the "Profession de foi du vicaire savoyard": the Deity has made man good and has implanted in him the moral energy to overcome the evils of a society that has not been built on natural principles. In this manner, Lanson argues, all parts of Rousseau's philosophy hold together, supplement each other, and express the central doctrine from which issues all the power of Rousseau's vision—the belief that man, by nature good, can transform himself into the good citizen in the good society.[57]

In a remarkable article on the unity of Rousseau's thought, published in 1912 on the occasion of Rousseau's bicentenary, Lanson

---

[53] Troisième Dialogue (Hachette ed., IX, 287). Cf. Lanson, *Histoire de la littérature française*, p. 769. Cf. below, p. 54.

[54] *Histoire de la littérature française*, p. 771.

[55] *Rousseau juge de Jean-Jacques,* Troisième Dialogue (Hachette ed., IX, 287). Cf. Lanson, *Histoire de la littérature française*, p. 769.

[56] *Ibid.*, p. 773.   [57] Cf. *ibid.*, pp. 774–75.

18

restated his position: We can indeed find contradictions of detail in Rousseau's work and we may point, if we please, to the unbridgeable gap between doctrine and life, but the general direction of his thought is constant and clear. Rousseau's problem, in the light of which all his writings can be grasped, is stated thus: "How can civilized man recover the benefits of the natural man, so innocent and happy, without returning to the state of nature, without renouncing the advantages of the social state?" [58] The early Discourses, then, are protests against all hitherto existing societies, whose evils they expose; *Emile* and the *Nouvelle Héloïse* point the way to the reform of the individual in the spheres of personal morality, family relations, and education; the later political writings outline the kind of society in which the good man can properly live. Cassirer fully agrees with Lanson's method, with his strictures of interpreters who "reduce each work of Rousseau to a simple and absolute formula," and with his conception of Rousseau's system as "a living thought which developed in the conditions of his life, exposed to all the vicissitudes and tumults of the atmosphere." [59]

Cassirer's essay had another brilliant predecessor, *The Meaning of Rousseau*, by E. H. Wright, who took the trouble to read all of Rousseau with care. Wright was appalled that as late as 1928 there should be "no document in English, and but few in any language," that attempted to find out simply what Rousseau meant to say. [60] His own method—like that of Lanson before, and of Cassirer after him—was straightforward: "In the effort to find out his doctrine, I have tried to ponder all his work together. If I am in error, I would ask to have it shown by an appeal to all his utterance rather than to an occasional flash of paradox." [61]

[58] "L'Unité de la pensée de Jean-Jacques Rousseau," *Annales de la Société Jean-Jacques Rousseau*, VIII (1912), 16.

[59] *Ibid.*, pp. 3, 7.   [60] *The Meaning of Rousseau*, p. v.

[61] *Ibid.*, p. vi.

Rousseau's underlying idea Wright found in "nature"—but nature interpreted in an unusual way.[62] "The idea," says Wright, "that man must be perfected by his reason in accordance with his nature runs through all of Rousseau's work and gives it an essential unity." [63] Accordingly, Wright expounds Rousseau's doctrine in chapters dealing with natural man, natural education, natural society, and natural religion. The natural man recognizes that "nature is right." But this does not mean that he must be an animal or a savage. Reason and conscience are part of man's nature, too—and, indeed, his better part. Nor does it mean that he must reject art and civilization: "All art is right which simply enlarges us, but none is right if it distorts us." The task of reason is to show man what is natural to him at a given stage of his development; the task of freedom is to enable him to act as he ought. Freedom can be meaningful only if we obey law, but a law to which we assent freely because we recognize its rationality: "When our will becomes autonomously one with principle we shall know the ultimate freedom." [64]

The role of natural education is to prevent the creation of a little tyrant or a little slave. We must let the child find the bounds of his own capacities for himself; we must reason with him only when he is old enough to reason—that is the only way to create

[62] Wright's stress on Rousseau's conception of nature is an important event in the history of Rousseau criticism. With the growing popularity of the scientific and the materialist outlooks after the seventeenth century, the conception of nature had undergone a steady transformation. The scientists defined nature as the lawful external world which man must understand; the materialists saw nature as a treasure house which man must exploit; Rousseau understood nature as "living nature," which Schiller was to call *beseelte Natur*—a moral force in which man participates or to which he aspires. Rousseau's conception thus included the idea of potentiality. Cf. Friedrich Schiller's important essay, *Über naive und sentimentalische Dichtung*, first published in 1795. (*Sämtliche Werke* [Leipzig: Tempel Verlag, n.d.], IV, 357–461.)

[63] *The Meaning of Rousseau*, p. 32.

[64] *Ibid.*, pp. 7, 24, 29. Wright recognizes what Cassirer later expounds—the close relationship of Kant's and Rousseau's ethics.

the natural man. Rousseau's political theory—the theory of the natural society—continues this theme. Men, such as they are now, are not fit for liberty. They must be made fit, and they must create for themselves a state that will make them so: "If the citizen must make the state, the state in turn must make true citizens." [65] Wright's position may be epitomized in one sentence: Rousseau is opposed to treating children as adults or adults as children.

Natural religion, finally, is the logical outgrowth of Rousseau's thought. Its object is to know God not through disputation or ritual but by the natural employment of reason in full concord with sentiment. "The natural religion . . . is the latest of religions to develop and the heir of all the others . . . the natural man is not our first brute forebear, but the last man whom we are travelling on to be." [66]

VI

This, in brief, was the state of the Rousseau literature when Ernst Cassirer published his essay, "Das Problem Jean Jacques Rousseau." Cassirer's eminence as historian of ideas and technical philosopher, combined with his neo-Kantianism, made him an ideal interpreter of Rousseau's work.[67] Kant, as Cassirer was fond of pointing out, had been almost the only eighteenth-century reader of Rousseau to prize him for his real rather than his alleged virtues.[68] Kant's ethical speculations had been profoundly enriched by Rousseau's philosophy, and Cassirer developed Kant's suggestive clue that the key to Rousseau lay in his rationalist conception of freedom.

Cassirer, whose critical method of *Verstehen* is brilliantly ex-

[65] *Ibid.*, p. 112.   [66] *Ibid.*, p. 164.

[67] See *The Philosophy of Ernst Cassirer* (Evanston: The Library of Living Philosophers, 1949), esp. James Gutmann, "Cassirer's Humanism," pp. 445–64.

[68] Cf. below, p. 58, and Cassirer's essay, "Kant and Rousseau," in *Rousseau, Kant, Goethe.*

emplified in his essay on Rousseau, held that the critic begins the process of understanding a philosopher's work by searching for a dynamic center of thought.[69] He must regard doctrines not as a series of discrete positions but as facets of a single point of view. The critic's equipment must therefore include the gift of empathy: he must sympathetically enter—indeed, relive—the thinker's world of ideas. More, he must imaginatively recreate, for himself if not for others, the environment in which the philosopher wrote and polemicized.

History and philosophy thus become inextricably intertwined; the interpreter who has immersed himself in Rousseau's world will not mistake Rousseau's attack on "culture" for an assault on all civilization whatever but will correctly see it as a criticism of the kind of civilization that Parisian society represented. At the same time, the critic will not indulge in reading into the doctrines of the man all the consequences drawn from them by others. *Verstehen* is a process which works only from the inside out. What Cassirer said about his approach to the philosophy of history—that his "aim [was] not to record and describe bare results, but rather to elucidate the inner formative forces" [70]—certainly applies to his study of Rousseau.

Once this point of view is understood, Cassirer's sophisticated use of biography becomes clearer. Cassirer did not despise the genetic method. Quite the contrary, his essay abounds with quota-

---

[69] Cassirer's method may be traced back to Wilhelm Dilthey, who himself was decisively influenced by Kant. For Dilthey's theory of interpretation, see *Gesammelte Schriften* (Leipzig: Teubner, 1914–36), Vol. I: *Einleitung in die Geisteswissenschaften;* Vol. VII: *Der Aufbau der geschichtlichen Welt in den Geisteswissenschaften;* and "Die Entstehung der Hermeneutik," in V, 317–38. See also the remarks of Harry Slochower in "Ernst Cassirer's Functional Approach to Art and Literature," in *The Philosophy of Ernst Cassirer*, p. 654, n. 30.

[70] *The Philosophy of the Enlightenment* (Princeton: Princeton University Press, 1951), p. vi. This book first appeared in German in 1932, the year in which the essay on Rousseau was published.

22

tions from Rousseau's *Confessions,* from the correspondence, and from *Rousseau juge de Jean-Jacques.* A genesis of Rousseau's work, Cassirer points out, is impossible "unless we trace that work back to its point of departure in Rousseau's life and to its roots in his personality. These two elements—the man and the work— are so closely interwoven that every attempt to disentangle them must do violence to both by cutting their common vital nerve. . . . Rousseau's fundamental thought, although it had its immediate origin in his nature and individuality, was neither circumscribed by nor bound to that individual personality." [71] The interpreter of Rousseau must use biographical data as significant points of departure, but he must not end with them; he must not confuse petty gossip about Rousseau's foibles with historical criticism.

Cassirer's method suggests, although it does not require, an approach to history and philosophy which places heavy stress on the study of the nature of man. Kant was deeply interested in problems of philosophical anthropology. So was Cassirer, whose *Philosophie der symbolischen Formen* is a monumental portrait of man as symbolizing, world-shaping animal.[72] And he did more than inquire into Rousseau's views on human nature—he emphasized that the search for the essence of man was among Rousseau's chief concerns.[73] Rousseau gave early proof of this preoccupation in the *Discours sur l'inégalité;* late in life he was to describe himself as "the historian of human nature," [74] recalling Hobbes's definition of the study of man: "To read in himself, not this or that particular man; but mankind."

[71] Cf. below, pp. 39–40.

[72] An English translation, by Ralph Manheim, has now been completed: *The Philosophy of Symbolic Forms,* 3 vols. (New Haven: Yale University Press, 1953-1957).

[73] Cf. below, p. 65.

[74] *Rousseau juge de Jean-Jacques,* Troisième Dialogue (Hachette ed., IX, 288).

In the hands of a philosopher like Cassirer, this imaginative method helps to reveal the principles that give coherence to a system of ideas. But the essay on Rousseau suggests difficulties in its application. The assiduous search for an intellectual core may sweep away, as insignificant, contradictions which are actually fundamental. The urge of Idealism toward unity and comprehensiveness may tend to reconcile in a supposedly higher synthesis that which is really irreconcilable. It is indeed possible to argue that Cassirer imposes more system on Rousseau than is actually present and that, in his emphasis on "freedom," he makes more of a Kantian of Rousseau than the facts warrant.[75] Moreover, Cassirer's rationalist approach to biography is open to criticism. I do not mean to suggest that the critic should psychoanalyze the author whose work he is assessing—such a procedure is often irrelevant and sometimes pernicious. But a critic who, like Cassirer, relies on biography cannot afford to neglect completely the contributions of Freud and of the discipline which he founded.

Despite these reservations, Cassirer's essay is an aesthetic as well as intellectual achievement of the first order. Its argument unfolds before us with measured pace, and the reader feels its full power only at the conclusion, when the whole chain of proof, which has been so carefully welded together, can be grasped and tested and is found to hold firm.

VII

Did Cassirer's essay succeed in solving the problem it set before itself? Several of the most significant books on Rousseau that have appeared since 1932 show and acknowledge its impact.[76]

[75] That, at any rate, is the conclusion of Robert Derathé: "A vouloir faire de sa doctrine une sorte de kantisme avant la lettre, on finit par la dénaturer ou la mutiler. M. Cassirer n'est pas tout à fait à l'abri de ce reproche." *Le Rationalisme de J.-J. Rousseau* (Paris: Presses Universitaires, 1948), p. 188.

[76] In the same year in which Cassirer's essay appeared he presented his point

Perhaps the most important of these publications is Charles W. Hendel's *Jean-Jacques Rousseau Moralist,* which specifically affirms the "very closest agreement" with Cassirer's "excellent discussions." [77] The point of Hendel's study, worked out in a detailed intellectual biography, is implicit in its title: Rousseau seeks to define the good life; his fundamental problem is "to set men free from their own tyranny, tyranny within as well as without." [78] In that light all his work can be seen to have consistency and unity. In the course of his exhaustive study Hendel took pains to refute other Rousseau interpretations, and Cassirer later paid tribute to Hendel's work.[79]

In recent years the Rousseau literature has been enriched by two contributions of Robert Derathé.[80] Unlike most commentators, Derathé believes that "the political theory of Rousseau emerged from his reflections on the theories held by the thinkers who belong to what has been called the *school of the law of nature and law of nations.*" [81] With great dexterity, M. Derathé traces the dependence of Rousseau on Grotius and Pufendorf, as well as on Hobbes and Locke. He makes a convincing case for a thesis for

of view in the form of a paper and subsequent discussion to the French Society of Philosophy. See Cassirer, "L'Unité dans l'œuvre de Jean-Jacques Rousseau," *Bulletin de la Société Française de Philosophie,* 32d year, No. 2 (April–June, 1932), pp. 46–66.

[77] C. W. Hendel, *Jean-Jacques Rousseau Moralist* (2 vols.; London: Oxford University Press, 1934), I, ix.

[78] *Ibid.,* II, 323.

[79] *Rousseau, Kant, Goethe,* p. 58n. In 1934 there appeared another volume worthy of note, Alfred Cobban's *Rousseau and the Modern State* (see note 6 above). Although it does not mention Cassirer specifically, its methods and conclusions are in the Lanson-Wright-Cassirer tradition.

[80] *Le Rationalisme de J.-J. Rousseau* (see note 75 above), and *Jean-Jacques Rousseau et la science politique de son temps* (Paris: Presses Universitaires, 1950). See Alfred Cobban's extensive review of both volumes, "New Light on the Political Thought of Rousseau," *Political Science Quarterly,* LXVI, No. 2 (June, 1951), 272–84.

[81] *Jean-Jacques Rousseau et la science politique de son temps,* p. 1.

which readers of Cassirer's essay are well prepared: that Rousseau belongs, in spirit, with the rationalist individualists whom he is supposed to have overcome and denied. Derathé considerably expands a number of points which Cassirer analyzed only briefly, and he illuminates Rousseau's treatment of the relation of conscience to reason and the development of reason in man. His conclusion is remarkably close to Cassirer's: "Rousseau never believed that one should fail to employ one's reason. . . . Quite to the contrary, he wanted to teach us how to use it well. . . . Rousseau is a rationalist aware of the limits of reason." [82] Derathé does not exempt Cassirer's essay from all criticism. In his view, Cassirer states his case for Rousseau's rationalism too strongly. Nevertheless, he calls the essay "much the most significant" of the neo-Kantian interpretations of Rousseau and "the most vigorous effort toward synthesis that has been undertaken up to now to seize the thought of Rousseau in its entirety and show in it a profound coherence." [83]

But influence apart, what can we say of Cassirer's achievement? A thinker is not a puzzle; he is never completely "solved." But Cassirer raised the question of Jean Jacques Rousseau to a new, higher plane. His essay beautifully illuminated the relation of Rousseau's fundamental conceptions to one another and to the rest of his thought—the relation of actual to potential reason, of perfectibility to the demand for a new society, of education to rationality, and most important, the relation of reason to freedom. Some critics have remained unconvinced;[84] yet if the portrayal of Rousseau the

[82] *Le Rationalisme de J.-J. Rousseau*, pp. 169, 176.

[83] *Ibid.*, pp. 181n, 185.

[84] E.g., Henri Peyre: "Rousseau is rife with contradictions, and the most ingenious men of learning (Lanson, Höffding, Schinz, and E. H. Wright) have not yet succeeded in convincing us of the unity of his thought." "The Influence of Eighteenth Century Ideas on the French Revolution," in *The Making of Modern Europe*, I, 482.

emotional, self-contradictory totalitarian has generally given way to a more accurate estimate, Cassirer's essay may claim a large share of the credit.

VIII

For Cassirer's reader the problem of Rousseau's political theory emerges in its true dimensions only after the fundamental unity of his philosophy has been firmly established. Its objective consistency, let it be repeated, is not affected by the fact that his political thought has served individualists and collectivists, libertarians and totalitarians. However, the relation of Rousseau's political theory to the historical process raises important questions which Cassirer's essay helps us to state properly but does not answer.

While a brief Introduction is not the place for a detailed inquiry into this relation, it may be useful to indicate the direction which such an inquiry might take. I would suggest, then, that we draw a distinction between Rousseau's political theory as a critical instrument and as a constructive device.[85] Used as a critical yardstick, Rousseau's political thought has been invaluable to democratic movements; used as a political blueprint, it has had a pernicious effect on libertarian ideas and institutions.

Rousseau's "one great principle"—that man is good, that society makes him bad, but that *only* society, the agent of perdition, can be the agent of salvation—is a *critical* tool. It affirms not only that reform is desirable but, more important, that it is possible, and it suggests that a society which creates only knaves and fools has forfeited its right to existence. But Rousseau is the philosopher of the democratic movement in an even more direct manner: throughout his writings he enumerates those features which make

[85] I am indebted to the late Franz Neumann of Columbia University for the formulation that Rousseau is the theorist of democratic movements but not of the democratic state.

contemporary society evil and those features by which we may recognize the opposite, the good society, in which the *volonté générale* is supreme. The greatest social evil is inequality: the greatest social good is freedom. Rousseau makes these points—two powerful weapons in the democratic armory—again and again, from his first Discourses to *Rousseau juge de Jean-Jacques*. His most significant statements in social theory are critical devices. We need to recall only his demand that the general will must be absolutely general ("All votes must be counted; any formal exclusion is a breach of generality" [86]); his criticism of representative government in which the sovereign people surrender what they ought to retain for themselves ("The moment a people gives itself representatives it is no longer free; it no longer exists" [87]); and his charge against French intellectual culture and the manners of his day—that they (like inequality) detract from, rather than enlarge, life.

For a party out of power or a philosopher in opposition, no theory could be more useful or consistent than Rousseau's. Once it is embodied in institutions, however, once the democratic party has gained power, the absolutist implications of his philosophy emerge. Rousseau attacks voluntary associations, deprecates dissent, wishes to impose a civil religion which can be disobeyed only on pain of exile or death. This is consistent with the rest of his thought: the kind of citizen he wants to create—the new man of *Emile* who must be so carefully shielded from the society of his own day lest he be corrupted by it—would not desire to belong to any special interest group; he would have no inclination to disagree with the decisions of the general will. Indeed, he would recognize the civil religion as a necessary cement and either believe in it or profess it without scruple. The supremacy of the

[86] *Contrat social*, Livre II, Chap. ii (Hachette ed., III, 319n).
[87] *Ibid.*, Livre III, Chap. xv (Hachette ed., III, 362).

volonté générale is a prescriptive demand, a moral claim made for the good man who does not yet exist but whom an equalitarian society and a natural education are to bring forth. Rousseau presupposes, as he himself says, "that all the qualities of the general will are still present in the majority: when they cease to be so . . . there will be no more freedom." [88]

It is this normative conception, this Utopian tendency to reason from the perfectibility of man to the perfect state in which only the perfect man can live, that makes Rousseau's thought so great as criticism and so dangerous when taken as a guide for constitution making. Rousseau's critical principles turn into fetters once the critic is transformed into the sovereign.

IX

That we are moved to speculate so freely about Rousseau's political theory after reading Cassirer is at once a tribute to the suggestive range of Cassirer's essay, and to the enduring fascination of Rousseau's political thinking. Cassirer was not himself a political theorist, but his work is supremely relevant to political theorists, who forget all too easily that political ideas evolve in a wider context.[89] Cassirer's essay stands as an enduring reminder that the po-

---

[88] *Ibid.*, Livre IV, Chap. ii (Hachette ed., III, 368). If we interpret the *Contrat social* in this manner, the supposed contradiction between it and the far less radical *Gouvernement de Pologne* is resolved: the former deals with men as they can and ought to be, the latter with men as they are.

[89] There is indeed one dimension of Rousseau's experience which Cassirer does not neglect but might well have expanded: Rousseau the citizen of Geneva. Some of Rousseau's most important writings, including the *Contrat social*, reflect Genevan party struggles and apply directly to Genevan realities. Fortunately, there are two fine books which illuminate the intimate ties of Rousseau's thought with the city of his birth: Gaspard Vallette, *Jean-Jacques Rousseau Genevois* (Paris and Geneva, 1911), and John Stephenson Spink, *Jean-Jacques Rousseau et Genève . . . pour servir d'introduction aux Lettres écrites de la montagne* (Paris, Boivin: 1934).

litical theorist who tears political writings from their context in the author's thought as a whole will mutilate their meaning. It is not an accident that the greatest political theorists have rarely been *merely* that; they have been primarily thinkers whose interest in man and in the universe included man's relation to the state. When Aristotle describes his *Politics* as the continuation of his *Ethics,* when Hobbes thinks it essential to devote sixteen chapters of the *Leviathan* to "Man" before proceeding to "Commonwealth," these are hints which the reader should respect and the interpreter should take seriously.

Cassirer did take them seriously. He was at one with Samuel Johnson, who once wrote about poetry: "Parts are not to be examined till the whole has been surveyed; there is a kind of intellectual remoteness necessary for the comprehension of any great work in its full design and in its true proportions; a close approach shows the smaller niceties, but the beauty of the whole is discerned no longer."

NOTE ON THE TEXT

Ernst Cassirer's essay, "Das Problem Jean Jacques Rousseau," first appeared in the *Archiv für Geschichte der Philosophie,* XLI (1932), 177–213, 479–513. On February 27, 1932, in an address on "L'Unité dans l'œuvre de Jean-Jacques Rousseau" before the Société Française de Philosophie (followed by a discussion), Cassirer presented the substance of his essay in French. Cf. *Bulletin de la Société Française de Philosophie,* 32d year, No. 2 (April–June, 1932), pp. 46–66.

"Das Problem Jean Jacques Rousseau" never appeared in book form in its original German version, but an Italian translation came out as a small book: *Il problema Gian Giacomo Rousseau,* translated by Maria Albanese (Florence: La Nuova Italia, 1938). The present version is the first to appear in English. It may be noted, however, that some brief passages from the essay are contained in Cassirer's *The Philosophy of the Enlightenment,* translated by Fritz C. A. Koelln and James P. Pettegrove (Princeton: Princeton University Press, 1951), as well as in his later essay, "Kant and Rousseau," in *Rousseau, Kant, Goethe,* translated by James Gutmann, Paul Oskar Kristeller, and John Herman Randall, Jr., (Princeton: Princeton University Press, 1945).

In this edition, I have attempted to stay as close to Cassirer's meaning and style as English usage would permit. The few typographical errors have been quietly corrected, and Cassirer's lengthy paragraphs have been divided, but beyond this no changes have been made.

Cassirer's practice concerning quotations from the French was not uniform—at least not in this essay. Some passages he translated, others he left in the original. Whenever Cassirer rendered a French quotation into German, I have translated it into English in the text; whenever he left it in French, I followed his practice and put the English translation into a footnote.

In all but one case (the quotation on pp. 86–88), I have translated directly from the original source rather than from Cassirer's German version. All translations from the French are my own, except for the verse translations, which are the work of my editor, J. Christopher Herold.

Cassirer followed the practice of shortening quotations by omitting words, phrases, or whole sentences, frequently without indicating the fact—but never, be it added, distorting the sense. Some of these omissions have been restored, and the omissions of longer passages have been indicated by the usual method of suspension points enclosed in square brackets. References have been made to the Hachette edition of Rousseau's works (which has been reprinted frequently in the second half of the nineteenth

31

century and at the beginning of the twentieth), since it is far more accessible than the edition which Cassirer used. This edition, it would seem, is the one listed by Jean Sénelier, *Bibliographie générale des œuvres de J.-J. Rousseau* (Paris: Presses Universitaires de France, 1949), under No. 1,901: *Collection des œuvres complèttes (sic) de J.-J. Rousseau,* Chez Sanson, Aux Deux Ponts [Zweibrücken], 1782–84, 30 vols. in 12mo.

Cassirer's own footnotes have been left unchanged except for minor matters of style. In the footnotes as in the text, all my additions are enclosed in square brackets. No attempt has been made to cite Rousseau's individual works by their full titles; the generally accepted shortened titles have been used—e.g., *Discours sur les sciences et les arts*. The spelling of French quotations has been modernized.

THE QUESTION OF
JEAN-JACQUES ROUSSEAU

1

I SHALL SPEAK of the question of Jean-Jacques Rousseau. Yet the very formulation of this topic implies a certain assumption—the assumption that Rousseau's personality and world of ideas have not been reduced to a mere historical fact that leaves us no further task but to comprehend it and describe it in its simple actuality. Even today, we do not think of Rousseau's doctrine as of an established body of single propositions that can be easily recorded and fitted into histories of philosophy by means of textual reproduction and review. True, that is how innumerable monographs have described it; but compared with Rousseau's own work all these accounts seem peculiarly cold and lifeless.

Anyone who penetrates deeply into this work and who reconstructs from it a view of Rousseau the man, the thinker, the artist, will feel immediately how little the abstract scheme of thought that is customarily given out as "Rousseau's teaching" is capable of grasping the inner abundance that is revealed to us. What is disclosed to us here is not fixed and definite doctrine. It is, rather, a movement of thought that ever renews itself, a movement of such strength and passion that it seems hardly possible in its presence to take refuge in the quiet of "objective" historical contemplation. Again and again it forces itself upon us; again and again it carries us away with it. The incomparable power which Rousseau the thinker and writer exercised over his time was ultimately founded in the fact that in a century that had raised the cultivation of form to unprecedented heights, bringing it to perfection and organic completion, he brought once more to the fore the inherent uncertainty of the very concept of form. In its literature as well as in its philosophy and science, the eighteenth century had come to rest in a fixed and definite world of forms. The reality of things was rooted in this world; their worth was determined and guaranteed by it. The century rejoiced in the unmistakable precision of things, in their clear and sharp outlines and firm boundaries, and it viewed the faculty of drawing such precise boundaries as the highest subjective strength of man and at the same time as the basic power of reason.

Rousseau was the first thinker who not only questioned this certainty but who shook its very foundations. He repudiated and destroyed the molds in which ethics and politics, religion as well as literature and philosophy were cast—at the risk of letting the world sink back once more into its primordial shapelessness, into the state of "nature," and thus of abandoning it, as it were, to chaos. But in the midst of this chaos which he himself had conjured up, his peculiar creative power was tested and proved. For now there commenced a movement animated by new impulses and determined by new forces. The aims of this movement remained, at first, in the dark; they could not be characterized in abstract isolation or anticipated as settled and given points of destination. When Rousseau attempted such anticipations he never got beyond vague and frequently contradictory formulations. What was settled for him, what he grasped at with the fullest strength of thought and feeling, was not the goal toward which he was steering but the impulse which he was following. And he dared to surrender to this impulse: he opposed the essentially static mode of thought of the century with his own completely personal dynamics of thought, feeling, and passion. His dynamics still holds us enthralled today. Even for us,

36

Rousseau's doctrine is not the object of mere academic curiosity nor of purely philological or historical examination. As soon as we cease to be content with examining its results and, instead, concern ourselves with its fundamental assumptions, his doctrine appears rather as a thoroughly contemporary and living means of approaching problems. The questions which Rousseau put to his century have by no means become antiquated; they have not been simply "disposed of"—even for us. Their *formulation* may frequently be significant and comprehensible only in a historical sense: their *content* has lost nothing of its immediacy.

That this should be so is in a large measure the result of the ambiguous portrait that purely historical inquiry has painted. After the most thorough research into biographical detail, after the countless investigations into the historical background and sources of Rousseau's doctrine, after the penetrating analysis of his writings that has extended to every detail, we should expect that clarity would have been achieved at least in regard to the basic characteristics of his nature or that a consensus would prevail concerning the basic intention of his work. But even a glance at the Rousseau literature disappoints this expectation. Particularly in recent years this colossal literature has been increased by several important and voluminous works. But if we look at these works —if we compare, for example (to mention only the most important names), the most recent account of Rousseau in Albert Schinz's book, *La Pensée de Jean-Jacques Rousseau* (Paris, 1929), with the accounts by Hubert and Masson [1]—the sharpest conflict in interpretation becomes obvious at once. This conflict is not confined to details and nonessentials; it concerns, rather, the

[1] [René] Hubert, *Rousseau et l'Encyclopédie: essai sur la formation des idées politiques de Rousseau* (Paris, 1928); [Pierre-Maurice] Masson, *La Religion de J.-J. Rousseau* (3 vols.; Paris, 1916). Cf. esp. the critique of Masson's views in [Albert] Schinz, "La Pensée religieuse de Jean-Jacques Rousseau et ses récents interprètes," *Smith College Studies in Modern Languages*, Vol. X, No. 1 (1928).

fundamental conception of Rousseau's nature and outlook. At times, Rousseau is portrayed as the true pioneer of modern individualism, a man who championed the unfettered liberty of feeling and the "right of the heart" and who conceived of this right so loosely that he completely abandoned every ethical obligation, every objective precept of duty. Karl Rosenkranz, for example, holds that Rousseau's morality "is the morality of the natural man who has not raised himself to the objective truth of self-determination through obedience to the moral law. In its subjective capriciousness it does both good and, occasionally, evil; but it tends to represent the evil as a good because the evil supposedly has its origin in the feeling of the good heart." [2] But it is precisely the opposite reproach which is usually leveled against Rousseau, certainly with no less justice. He is seen as the founder and champion of a state socialism which completely sacrifices the individual to the group and forces him into a fixed political order within which he finds neither freedom of activity nor even freedom of conscience.

Opinions concerning Rousseau's religious beliefs and orientation diverge as widely as those concerning his ethical and political beliefs. The "Profession de foi du vicaire savoyard" in *Emile* has been most variously interpreted. Some have seen in it a high point of eighteenth-century Deism. Others have called attention to its close ties to "positive" religion and have laid bare the threads which connect this "Profession" with the Calvinist faith in which Rousseau grew up.[3] And the most recent comprehensive account of Rousseau's religion, in Masson's *La Religion de Jean-Jacques Rousseau,* does not flinch from the paradox of fitting Rousseau's religious feeling and outlook entirely into the sphere of Cathol-

[2] Karl Rosenkranz, *Diderot's Leben und Werke* (Leipzig, 1866), II, 75.

[3] Rousseau's fundamentally Protestant-Calvinist outlook is emphasized by, among others, [Gustave] Lanson. Cf. his *Histoire de la littérature française,* 22d ed. (Paris: Hachette, 1930), pp. 788ff.

icism and of claiming him for it. According to Masson, there exists a real, deep, all-too-long neglected connection not only between Rousseau and religion but between Rousseau and the Catholic faith.

The attempt to measure Rousseau's world of ideas by the traditional antithesis of "rationalism" and "irrationalism" results in equally ambiguous and uncertain judgments. That Rousseau turned away from the glorification of reason that prevailed in the circle of the French Encyclopedists, that he appealed, instead, to the deeper forces of "feeling" and "conscience"—all this is undeniable. On the other hand, it was precisely this "irrationalist" who, at the height of his struggle against the *philosophes* and the spirit of the French Enlightenment, coined the phrase that the loftiest ideas that man could form of the Deity were purely and exclusively grounded in reason: "Les plus grandes idées de la divinité nous viennent par la raison seule." [4] Furthermore, it was this "irrationalist" whom no less a man than Kant compared with Newton and called the Newton of the moral world.

If we consider these divergences of judgment, we will immediately recognize that a true elucidation of Rousseau's nature can neither be gained nor be expected from these categories. We can achieve it only if we turn once more, untouched by all prejudgments and prejudices, to Rousseau's work itself—if we let it come into being before our eyes in accord with its own inner law.

However, such a genesis of his work is not possible unless we trace that work back to its point of departure in Rousseau's life and to its roots in his personality. These two elements—the man and the work—are so closely interwoven that every attempt to disentangle them must do violence to both by cutting their

[4] ["Profession de foi du vicaire savoyard," in *Emile*, Livre IV (Hachette ed., II, 267).]

common vital nerve. True, it is not my purpose to maintain that Rousseau's world of ideas lacks independent meaning apart from his individual form of existence and personal life. It is rather the opposite hypothesis I want to defend here. What I shall try to show is this: that Rousseau's fundamental thought, although it had its immediate origin in his nature and individuality, was neither circumscribed by nor bound to that individual personality; that in its maturity and perfection this thought puts before us an objective formulation of questions; and that this formulation is valid not for him or his era alone but contains, in full sharpness and definiteness, an inner, strictly objective necessity. But this necessity does not stand immediately before us in abstract generality and systematic isolation. It emerges very gradually from the individual first cause of Rousseau's nature, and it must first, as it were, be liberated from this first cause; it must be conquered step by step. Rousseau always resisted the notion that a thought could have objective value and validity only when it appeared from the outset in systematically articulated and armor-plated form; he angrily rejected the idea that he should submit to such systematic compulsion. Rousseau's objection holds in the theoretical as well as in the practical spheres; it holds for the development of thought as well as the conduct of life. With a thinker of this sort the content and meaning of the work cannot be separated from the foundation of personal life; each can be comprehended only with the other and in the other, in repeated reflection and mutual illumination.

Rousseau's independent spiritual development began only at the moment of his arrival in Paris, when he was nearly thirty. Here, for the first time, he experienced the true awakening of his intellectual self-awareness. From that moment childhood and adolescence lay behind him, cloaked in blurred dimness. They remained for him only as objects of memory and of yearning—a yearning, it is true, which was to haunt Rousseau till his old age and never lost its power. What made Rousseau return again and again to the first impressions of his Swiss homeland was the feeling that there, and there alone, he had still possessed life as a true entity, as an unbroken whole. The break between the demands of the world and the demands of the self had not yet taken place; the power of feeling and imagination had not yet found a fixed and harsh boundary in the reality of things. Accordingly, both worlds, the world of the self and the world of things, were not yet sharply separated in Rousseau's consciousness. His boyhood and youth were a peculiarly fantastic tissue, strangely woven together from dream and reality, experience and imagination. His most complete, his richest and most "real" moments were not the moments of action and accomplishment but those hours in which he could forget and leave behind all reality, lost in the dream world of his fantasies, feelings, and desires. In week-long, aimless wanderings, roaming about freely, he sought and found this happiness again and again.

But the moment he entered Paris, this world sank from sight as with a single blow. Here another order of things awaited and received him—an order that allowed no scope to subjective arbitrariness and imagination. The day belonged to a mass of activities, and they controlled it down to the last detail. It was a day of work and of conventional social duties, each of which had its proper time and hour. This fixity of time regulation, of objective time measurement, was the first thing to which Rousseau had to become accustomed. From now on he had to do constant battle with this requirement, so alien to his nature. The rigid framework of time, determining man's ordinary working day and dominating him completely, this externally imposed and externally enforced budgeting of life, always appeared to Rousseau as an unbearable restraint on living. He could accomplish the most varied things and he could adjust himself to much that was really unsuitable to him, so long as the *time* for his activity was not prescribed along with the *kind*.

In that keen examination of his own nature, the dialogues to which he gave the characteristic title *Rousseau juge de Jean-Jacques,* Rousseau dwells expressly on this trait. Jean-Jacques, as he describes himself here, "loves activity, but he detests constraint. Work is no strain on him provided he can do it at his own rather than at another's time. [. . .] Must he accomplish some business, pay a visit, or take a trip? He will go to it at once if he is not pressed. If he is compelled to act immediately he becomes refractory. It was one of the happiest moments of his life when, renouncing all plans for the future in order to live from day to day, he got rid of his watch. 'Thank heavens!' he exclaimed in a transport of joy, 'I shall no longer need to know what time it is!' " [5]

To this revulsion against any regimentation and stereotyping of external life, Rousseau now added another feeling, deeper and more heartfelt, which estranged him more and more from traditional forms of sociability and drove him into himself. Shortly after his arrival it appeared that he might be able to adjust himself to these forms. During this time he was by no means the misanthropic hermit. He sought acquaintances and—especially in his friendship with Diderot, who was, so to speak, the personification of all vigorous spiritual forces of contemporary France—he found the tie which bound him firmly to the sociable and literary life of the time. Then, too, the personal reception which Rousseau got in Paris seemed destined, indeed expressly designed, gradually to divert his obstinacy into other paths and to lead to a reconciliation

[5] *Rousseau juge de Jean-Jacques,* Deuxième Dialogue (*Œuvres compl.* éd. Aux Deux-Ponts [Zweibrücken], 1782, p. 8) [Hachette ed., IX, 225]. Cf. *Confessions,* Livre VIII.

between him and the *esprit public*. Everywhere people were eager to extend him a friendly welcome. The Paris of that time was the acme and the zenith of courtly culture, and the characteristic virtue of this culture consisted of that exquisite courtesy with which every stranger was treated.

But it was precisely this pervasive courtesy, taken as a matter of course, which hurt and repelled Rousseau. For he learned, ever more clearly, to see through it to the bottom; he felt ever more strongly that this sort of friendliness knew no personal friendship. Rousseau has given the most intense description of this feeling in the letter of the *Nouvelle Héloïse* in which Saint-Preux relates his entry into Paris society. Here nothing is "invented"; every word is drawn from his own immediate experience. "I have been very warmly welcomed," writes Saint-Preux. "People meet me full of friendship; they show me a thousand civilities; they render me services of all sorts. But that is precisely what I am complaining of. How can you become immediately the friend of a man whom you have never seen before? The true human interest, the plain and noble effusion of an honest soul—these speak a language far different from the insincere demonstrations of politeness [and the false appearances] which the customs of the great world demand. I am very much afraid that the man who treats me as a friend of twenty years' standing at the first meeting could treat me in twenty years as a stranger if I had to ask him for some important favor; and when I discover in these [dissipated] people such a tender interest in so many persons I would gladly believe that they are not interested in anybody." [6]

Such was Rousseau's first impression of Paris society, and this impression continued to work in him and to deepen incessantly. We must seek the real source of his misanthropy at this point—

[6] *Nouvelle Héloïse*, Seconde Partie, Lettre xiv [Hachette ed., IV, 158].

a misanthropy which grew out of a genuine and deep feeling of love, out of the yearning for unconditional devotion and an enthusiastic ideal of friendship. It is the misanthropy which the most profound judge and painter of men in classical French literature described in an incomparable character. In the midst of the amiable and officious, the courtly and courteous world of Paris society, Rousseau was seized by that feeling of complete isolation which Molière has his Alceste express:

> Non, non, il n'est point d'âme un peu bien située
> Qui veuille d'une estime aussi prostituée.
>
> . . . .
>
> Sur quelque préférence une estime se fonde,
> Et c'est n'estimer rien qu'estimer tout le monde.
>
> . . . .
>
> Je refuse d'un cœur la vaste complaisance
> Qui ne fait de mérite aucune différence.
>
> . . . .
>
> J'entre en une humeur noire, en un chagrin profond,
> Quand je vois vivre entre eux les hommes comme ils font.
> Je ne trouve partout que lâche flatterie
> Qu'injustice, intérêt, trahison, fourberie;
> Je n'y puis plus tenir, j'enrage; et mon dessein
> Est de rompre en visière à tout le genre humain.[7]

[7] [*Le Misanthrope*, Act I, Scene 1:

> No, by esteem thus cheaply prostituted
> No well-bred soul could wish to be polluted.
>
> . . . .
>
> Esteem is based on preference of some kind:
> He values none who values all mankind.
>
> . . . .
>
> I spurn the easy friendship of a heart
> To whom all merit is of equal sort.
>
> . . . .
>
> I am all melancholy, sad, and blue
> When I behold men acting as they do.
> Where'er I turn, base flattery I see,
> Injustice, greed, deceit, and villainy.

But it was a different, a stronger impulse that drove Rousseau to this break. The same fundamental defect which he had earlier recognized in society he now recognized in its intellectual spokesmen as well, in the representatives of its true and most refined spirituality. This spirituality was as far removed from the genuine spirit of truth as the agreeable morals of the time were removed from true morality. For philosophy had long since forgotten how to speak its native language, the language of the teaching of wisdom. Now it only spoke the language of the time, fitting itself into the thought and interests of the era. The worst and harshest constraint of society lies in this power which it wields not only over our external actions but also over all our inner urges, all our thoughts and judgments. This power thwarts all independence, all freedom and originality of judgment. It is no longer we who think and judge: society thinks in us and for us. We no longer need search for the truth: it is pressed into our hand, fresh from the mint.

Rousseau describes this spiritual condition in his first philosophical essay. "There prevails in our morals an abject and deceptive uniformity, and all minds seem to have been cast in the same mold. Endlessly, politeness makes demands, decorum gives orders; endlessly, we follow customs, never our own bent. We no longer dare seem what we are; and, in this perpetual constraint the men who form this herd which we call society will all do the same things under the same circumstances." [8] Sociable man, constantly living outside himself, knows how to live only in the opin-

---

It is too much, I rage, and my desire
Is to defy the human race entire.

For Rousseau's own views concerning this play and, particularly, the character of Alceste, cf. his *Lettre à M. d'Alembert sur son article "Genève" dans l'Encyclopédie* (Hachette ed., I, 201–6).]

[8] *Premier Discours* [*Discours sur les sciences et les arts*], Première Partie [Hachette ed., I, 4].

ion of others, and can gather the awareness of his own existence solely through this derived and indirect method, by this round-about path of the opinion of others.[9]

But with these last sentences, which belong to Rousseau's second philosophical work, the *Discours sur l'origine de l'in-égalité,* we have already anticipated a later stage of his develop-ment. Let us turn back from it, in order to focus our eyes on the moment which we can describe as the actual hour of birth of Rousseau's fundamental thought. He himself has given us an incomparable and unforgettable description of it. It was on that summer's day of the year 1749, when Rousseau started from Paris to visit his friend Diderot, who had been confined in the Tower of Vincennes on the strength of a *lettre de cachet.* Rousseau was carrying an issue of the *Mercure de France* and, as he glanced through it while walking, his eyes suddenly fell on a prize question set by the Academy of Dijon for the next year. "Has the restoration of the sciences and the arts," so ran the question, "helped to purify morals?"

"If anything ever resembled a sudden inspiration," thus Rous-seau describes this moment in a letter to Malesherbes, "it was the emotion that worked in me as I read that. Of a sudden I felt my spirit dazzled by a thousand lights; swarms of [lively] ideas presented themselves to me at once, with a force [and confusion] that threw me into an inexpressible turmoil; I felt my head seized with a dizziness like that of inebriation. A violent palpitation oppressed me and made my chest heave. Since I could no longer breathe [while walking,] I let myself drop under one of the trees [by the wayside], and there I spent half an hour in such excitement that as I rose I noticed that [the whole front of] my jacket was wet with my [own] tears which I had shed without noticing it.

[9] [Cf.] *Discours sur l'origine de l'inégalité* (near the end) [Hachette ed., I, 126].

Oh, [Sir] if I could ever have written one fourth of what I had seen and felt under that tree, with what clarity I should have revealed all the contradictions of the social system! With what force I should have exposed all the abuses of our institutions! With what ease I should have shown that man is naturally good, and that it is through these institutions alone that men become bad. All I have been able to retain of those swarms of great truths that enlightened me [in a quarter of an hour] under that tree has been scattered quite feebly in my [three] main works, [namely, in that first *Discourse,* in the one on *Inequality,* and in the *Treatise on Education*]." [10]

The event which Rousseau describes in this letter had taken place more than a decade earlier, but we feel with every word how the memory still affects and shakes him with undiminished force. Indeed it was that moment which decided his personal fate as a thinker. The question that suddenly confronted him focused all doubts which had previously assailed him on one point. His suppressed indignation against all that his epoch loved and revered, against the eighteenth century's ideals of life and of culture, now broke out in him like a boiling stream of lava. For a long time Rousseau had felt estranged from these ideals; still, he had hardly dared to confess this to himself, much less give it visible expression. The splendor of the spiritual civilization in whose center he stood had still dazzled him; the friendship with the leaders of the spiritual movement, with Condillac and Diderot, had still held him back.

[10] Seconde Lettre à Malesherbes, Montmorency, 12 janvier 1762 [Hachette ed., X, 301–2]. The inner truthfulness of this account strikes us immediately. Over against it, Diderot's report to the effect that *he* had given Rousseau the fundamental idea of his essay in a conversation loses all weight. This can only have been a misunderstanding or a trick of memory on the part of Diderot. For a more detailed discussion of the question, see [John] Morley, *Diderot and the Encyclopaedists* (1878; new ed., London, 1923), I, 112f. [It is worth noting that this question is still the subject of discussion.]

But now all these laboriously constructed dams collapsed. A new ethical passion had awakened in him; irresistibly it drew from him a flood of new ideas. Now the inner tension which he had hitherto felt but vaguely and dimly became a distinct and certain knowledge. At a stroke, his feeling became clear and clairvoyant. Rousseau now *saw* where he stood; he not only felt, but he judged and condemned. He was not yet able to clothe this judgment in the form of philosophical conception and argumentation. If we consider his answer to the prize question of the Academy of Dijon from the philosophic and systematic point of view, the weaknesses and gaps in the chain of proof emerge throughout. As he looked back upon his first philosophical work, Rousseau did not conceal these weaknesses from himself. In a prefatory remark to a later edition of the *Discours* he points to the tragic irony that a work which does not bear comparison in content with any of his later writings should have laid the foundations of his literary fame. Indeed, the first *Discours* appears as a rhetorical masterpiece unsurpassed in the whole of Rousseau's writings; but in many respects it has remained a mere rhetorical display piece. And this rhetoric has lost its hold on us; it no longer has the overwhelming power over us that it had on his contemporaries. But no matter how we feel about it and about the single steps of Rousseau's argumentation, the truthfulness of Rousseau's inner sentiment impresses itself upon us in every sentence of the *Discours*. In every word there lives the urge to be rid of all oppressive learning, to shake off all the burden and splendor of knowledge in order to find the way back to the natural and simple forms of existence. Rousseau's ethics resolves itself into this one fundamental idea and feeling. "O Virtue! Sublime science of simple souls, are such labor and preparation necessary before we can know you? Are not your principles engraved on every heart? To learn your laws, is it not enough to return to

48

ourselves and to listen to the voice of our conscience in the silence of the passions? This is the true philosophy; we must know enough to be content with it, without envying the fame of the celebrated men who have become immortals in the republic of letters." [11]

When Rousseau demanded the "return to nature" in *this* sense— when he distinguished between what man is and what he has artificially made of himself, he derived the right to make this contrast neither from the knowledge of nature nor from the knowledge of history. For him both elements were of strictly subordinate significance. He was neither historian nor ethnologist, and it seemed to him a strange self-deception to hope that man might be changed and brought nearer to his "natural state" by historical or ethnological knowledge.

Rousseau was neither the only nor the first man in the eighteenth century to coin the motto, "Back to Nature!" Rather, its sound was to be heard everywhere, in inexhaustible variations. Descriptions of the customs of primitive peoples were eagerly snatched up; there was a mounting urge to acquire a wider view of primitive forms of life. Hand in hand with this new knowledge—mainly derived from travelers' reports—went a new feeling. Diderot made a report of Bougainville on his trip to the South Seas his starting point for celebrating with lyrical exaggeration the simplicity, the innocence, and the happiness of primitive peoples.[12] In Raynal's *Histoire philosophique et politique des établissemens et du commerce des Européens dans les deux Indes* (1772) the eighteenth century found an inexhaustible mine of information about "exotic" conditions and an arsenal for their enthusiastic praise. When Rousseau wrote the *Discours sur l'origine de l'inégalité,* this movement was already fully under way; but

[11] [*Discours sur les sciences et les arts,* Seconde Partie (Hachette ed., I, 20).]
[12] Diderot, *Supplément au Voyage de Bougainville* (written 1772).

he himself seems hardly touched by it. He made it unmistakably clear right at the beginning of that essay that he neither could nor wanted to describe a historically demonstrable original state of mankind. "Let us begin then by setting aside all the facts, since they do not affect the question. We must not take the researches which we may undertake concerning this subject as historical truths but only as hypothetical [and conditional] observations, more appropriate to throw light on the nature of things than to show their real origins." [13] The "nature of things" is present to us everywhere—to understand it we need not retrace our steps through the millennia, to the sparse and undependable evidence of prehistoric times. As Rousseau puts it in the preface to the *Discours sur l'inégalité:* The man who speaks of the "state of nature" speaks of a state which no longer exists, *which may never have existed, and which probably never will exist.* It is a state of which we must, nevertheless, have an adequate idea in order to judge correctly our present condition.[14]

The expansion of the spatial-geographic horizon can help us as little as the road back to prehistory. Whatever data we might gather in this area remain mute witnesses unless we find in ourselves the means of making them speak. The true knowledge of man cannot be found in ethnography or ethnology. There is only one living source for this knowledge—the source of self-knowledge and genuine self-examination. And it is to this alone that Rousseau appeals; from it he seeks to derive all proofs of his principles and hypotheses. In order to distinguish the *"homme naturel"* from the *"homme artificiel,"* we need neither go back to epochs of the distant and dead past nor take a trip around the world. Everyone carries the true archetype within himself; still, hardly anyone has been fortunate enough to discover it and to

[13] [Hachette ed., I, 83.]   [14] [Cf. Hachette ed., I, 79.]

strip it of its artificial wrappings, its arbitrary and conventional trimmings.

It is *this* discovery on which Rousseau prided himself and which he proclaimed to his age as his true accomplishment. All he could set against the scholarship, learning, philosophy, and political and sociological theories of his time was the simple testimony of his self-awareness and self-experience. Whence could the originator of this doctrine, as Rousseau writes in his *Rousseau juge de Jean-Jacques,* "whence could the painter and apologist of human nature, [today so defamed and maligned,] have taken his model, if not from his own heart? He has described this nature just as he felt it within himself. The prejudices which had not subjugated him, the artificial passions which had not made him their victim—they did not hide from his eyes, as from those of all others, the basic traits of humanity, so generally forgotten and misunderstood. [. . .] In a word, it was necessary that one man should paint his own portrait to show us, in this manner, the natural man; and if the author had not been just as singular as his books, he would never have written them. But where is he, this natural man who lives a truly human life; who, caring nothing for the opinions of others, acts only in accord with his impulses and reason, without regard for the praise or blame of society? In vain do we seek him among us. Everywhere only a varnish of words; all men seek their happiness in appearance. No one cares for reality, everyone stakes his essence on illusion. Slaves and dupes of their self-love, men live not in order to live but to make others believe that they have lived!" [15]

With these words and the disposition they express, Rousseau seems to profess an unfettered individualism; angrily he seems to cast off the burden of society once and for all. Up to this point,

[15] *Rousseau juge de Jean-Jacques,* Troisième Dialogue [Hachette ed., IX, 288].

however, we have comprehended only one pole of his nature and only one goal of his thought. Shortly after the composition of the *Discours sur l'origine de l'inégalité* an almost inconceivable reversal occurred in his thinking. We are now led to a dramatic turning point which still astonishes his interpreters. Rousseau becomes the author of the *Contrat social:* he writes the code for the very society which he has rejected and castigated as the cause of all the depravity and unhappiness of mankind. And what does this code look like? We might expect that it would keep society within bounds as much as possible—that it would narrow and delimit its powers so carefully that any attack on individuality would be checked.

But such an "attempt to determine the limits of the state" [16] was far from Rousseau's mind. The *Contrat social* proclaims and glorifies a completely unbounded absolutism of the state. Every particular and individual will is shattered by the power of the *volonté générale*. The very act of joining the state signifies the complete renunciation of all particular desires. Man does not give himself to the state and to society without giving himself completely to both. We may speak of a real "unity" of the state only if the individuals are merged in this unity and disappear in it. No reservation is possible here: "L'aliénation se faisant sans réserve, l'union est aussi parfaite qu'elle peut l'être, *et nul associé n'a plus rien à réclamer.*" [17]

This omnipotence of the state in no way stops with the actions of men; it claims their beliefs as well and places them under the harshest constraint. Religion, too, is civilized and socialized. The

[16] [This is an allusion to Wilhelm von Humboldt's essay, *Ideen zu einem Versuch, die Grenzen der Wirksamkeit des Staats zu bestimmen* (completed in 1792, published posthumously in 1851).]

[17] *Contrat social*, Livre I, Chap. vi [Hachette ed., III, 313]. ["Since the alienation is made unconditionally, the union is as perfect as it can be, and no associate has anything more to claim." Italics added by Cassirer.]

concluding chapter of the *Contrat social* deals with the establishment of the *religion civile,* which is absolutely binding on all citizens. It permits the individual complete freedom with respect to those dogmas that are irrelevant to the form of communal life, but it establishes all the more relentlessly a list of articles of faith concerning which, on penalty of expulsion from the state, no doubt is permitted. The articles of faith include belief in the existence of an omnipotent and infinitely beneficent Deity, Providence, life after death, and a Last Judgment. Is it too harsh a verdict when Taine in his *Origines de la France contemporaine,* calls the *Contrat social* a glorification of tyranny, and when he describes Rousseau's state as a prison and a monastery? [18]

The solution of this fundamental contradiction seems impossible, and indeed the majority of interpreters have despaired of it.[19] Well-known works in the Rousseau literature—I only mention the names of Morley, Faguet, Ducros, Mornet—declare candidly that the *Contrat social* explodes the unity of Rousseau's work, that it implies a complete break with the philosophical outlook from which this work had originally sprung. But even admitting that such a break is possible, how can we explain that it remained so completely concealed from Rousseau himself? For into his old age Rousseau never tired of affirming and upholding the unity of his work. He did not see the *Contrat social* as an apostasy from the fundamental ideas he had advocated in his two essays on the prize questions of the Academy of Dijon; it was, rather, their consistent extension, their fulfillment and perfection.

[18] [*L'Ancien Régime* (Paris: Hachette, 1896), pp. 319, 321, 323, and *passim.*]

[19] However, the unity of Rousseau's thought has been defended in the recent literature—particularly by Hubert, who sees the center and focus of Rousseau's work not in the *Discours sur l'inégalité* but in the *Contrat social. Rousseau et l'Encyclopédie: essai sur la formation des idées politiques de Rousseau* (Paris, 1928). This unity has also been defended—but from different points of view—by Schinz, *La Pensée de J.-J. Rousseau* (Paris, 1929), and by Lanson, *op. cit.* [*Histoire de la littérature française*].

Never, as *Rousseau juge de Jean-Jacques* emphasizes, had the attack on the arts and sciences been designed to throw mankind back into its original barbarism. Never would he have been able to form such a strange and chimerical plan: "In his first writings it was necessary to destroy the illusion which fills us with an absurd admiration for the instruments of our unhappiness and to correct those false sets of values which heap honors upon pernicious talents and despise benevolent virtues. Everywhere he shows us humanity as better, [wiser,] and happier in its original state, and as blind, unhappy, and evil to the degree that it has departed from that state. [. . .]

"But human nature does not turn back. Once man has left it, he can never return to the time of innocence and equality. It was on this principle that he particularly insisted. [. . .] He has been obstinately accused of wishing to destroy the sciences and the arts [. . .] and to plunge humanity back into its original barbarism. Quite the contrary: he always insisted on the preservation of existing institutions, maintaining that their destruction would leave the vices in existence and remove only the means to their cure, putting plunder in the place of corruption." [20]

Given the present stage of human development—with which our work must begin if it is not to remain empty and illusory—how are we to resist *both* plunder and corruption? How can we build a genuine and truly human community without falling in the process into the evils and depravity of conventional society? This is the question to which the *Contrat social* addresses itself. The return to the simplicity and happiness of the state of nature is barred to us, but the path of *freedom* lies open; it can and must be taken.

[20] *Rousseau juge de Jean-Jacques,* Troisième Dialogue [Hachette ed., IX, 287]. [The translation, "instruments of our unhappiness," follows Cassirer's German translation. The edition of Rousseau used by Cassirer must have *misères* where the Hachette ed. has *lumières.*]

At this point, however, the interpreter is compelled to enter difficult and slippery ground, for of all of Rousseau's conceptions, his conception of freedom has been interpreted in the most divergent and contradictory ways. In the controversy that has been raging for nearly two centuries, the conception has almost completely lost its precision. It has been pulled hither and yon by the hatred or favor of the parties; it has been reduced to a mere political slogan which, glittering today in all the colors of the spectrum, has been made to serve the most divergent political goals.

But one thing may be said: Rousseau cannot be held responsible for this ambiguity and confusion. He defined, clearly and firmly, the specific meaning and true basic significance of his idea of freedom. To him freedom did not mean arbitrariness but the overcoming and elimination of all arbitrariness, the submission to a strict and inviolable law which the individual erects over himself. Not renunciation of and release from this law but free consent to it determines the genuine and true character of freedom. And that character is realized in the *volonté générale,* the will of the state. The state claims the individual completely and without reservations. However, in doing so it does not act as a coercive institution but only puts the individual under an obligation which he himself recognizes as valid and necessary, and to which he therefore assents for its sake as well as for his own.

Here lies the heart of the whole political and social problem. It is not a question of emancipating and liberating the individual in the sense of releasing him from the form and order of the community; it is, rather, a question of finding the kind of community that will protect every individual with the whole concerted power of the political organization, so that the individual in uniting himself with all others nevertheless obeys only himself in this act of union. "Each man, by giving himself to all, gives himself to nobody; and since there is no associate over whom he does not

55

acquire the same right that he has given the other over himself, he gains the equivalent of everything he has lost and more power to preserve what he has." [21] "As long as the subjects have to submit only to such conventions, they obey no one but their own will." [22] To be sure, with this they give up the independence of the state of nature, the *indépendance naturelle,* but they exchange it for real freedom, which consists in tying all men to the law.[23] And only then will they have become individuals in the higher sense— autonomous personalities. Rousseau did not hesitate for an instant in elevating this ethical conception of personality far above the mere state of nature. On this point his words are of such unmistakable clarity and precision as we should hardly expect of a writer who is generally considered a blind worshiper of "primitive man." Although by entering the community man deprives himself of several advantages which he had possessed in the state of nature, he gains by this step such a development of his faculties, such an awakening of his ideas and refinement of his feelings, that if the abuses of his new condition did not frequently degrade him below the state of nature, he would have to bless without cease the happy moment that wrested him from this state forever and made him a spiritual being and a man instead of a limited and stupid animal.[24]

It is true that the thesis which the *Discours sur l'inégalité* seems to defend is here finally abandoned. In the earlier essay the entrance into the realm of spirituality still appears as a kind of defection from the happy state of nature, as a kind of biological depravity. Thinking man is a depraved animal: "L'homme qui

[21] *Contrat social,* Livre I, Chap. vi [Hachette ed., III, 313].

[22] *Ibid.,* Livre II, Chap. iv [Hachette ed., III, 323].

[23] *Ibid.* [In the original printing of Cassirer's text, the quotation marks and source references for this and the two preceding citations are slightly misplaced. The errors, which are probably typographical, have been corrected here.]

[24] *Ibid.,* Livre I, Chap. viii [Hachette ed., III, 315–16].

médite est un animal dépravé." [25] Similarly, the essay on the arts and sciences had maintained that nature desired to protect man from knowledge—like an anxious mother who snatches a dangerous weapon from the hands of her child.[26] Was all this now lost and forgotten for Rousseau? Had he decided unconditionally for "spirit" and against nature, and had he exposed himself without misgivings to all its dangers, which he himself had seen so clearly and judged so ruthlessly? And what can explain and justify this new orientation? We can find this explanation only if we do not overlook the right link. Knowledge—that is the insight which Rousseau had now achieved—is without danger as long as it does not try to raise itself above life and to tear itself away from it, as long as it serves the order of life itself. Knowledge must claim no absolute primacy, for in the realm of spiritual values it is the ethical will that deserves primacy.

In the ordering of the human community, too, the firm and clear formation of the world of the will must precede the construction of the world of knowledge. Man must first find within himself the clear and established law before he can inquire into and search for the laws of the world, the laws of external things. Once this first and most urgent problem has been mastered, once the spirit has achieved true freedom in the order of the political and social world—then man may safely give himself up to the freedom of inquiry. Knowledge will no longer fall victim to mere *raffinement;* it will not soften or enervate man. It was only a false ethical order of things which had diverted knowledge into this direction and which had reduced it to a mere intellectual refinement, a kind of spiritual luxury. It will return to the right path by itself once this impediment has been removed. Spiritual liberty

[25] *Discours sur l'inégalité,* Première Partie [Hachette ed., I, 87].
[26] *Premier Discours* [*Discours sur les sciences et les arts*], Première Partie (near the end) [Hachette ed., I, 10].

profits man nothing without ethical liberty, but ethical liberty cannot be achieved without a radical transformation of the social order, a transformation that will wipe out all arbitrariness and that alone can help the inner necessity of law to victory.

This hymn to the law and to its unconditional universal validity runs through all of Rousseau's political writings, although he has been most thoroughly and most frequently misunderstood precisely on this point. Only one man correctly understood the inner cohesion of Rousseau's world of ideas. Kant alone became Rousseau's admiring disciple on this very point. The traditional conception and interpretation of Rousseau, however, here took another, exactly opposite, direction. As early as the eighteenth century, conceptions and interpretations stood sharply opposed to each other: following Kant's example, the *Genieperiode* lifted Rousseau on its shield and made him the patron of *its* interpretation of freedom. In this interpretation, freedom was invoked *against* the law; the meaning and purpose of freedom were to release man from the pressure and constraint of the law. "I am asked to squeeze my body into stays," exclaims Karl Moor, "and straitlace my will in laws. Law has perverted to snail's pace what might have been an eagle's flight. Never yet has law formed a great man, but freedom breeds giants and extremes." [27]

But this mood of the *Sturm und Drang* was not the fundamental intellectual and ethical disposition of Rousseau. For him, law is not an opponent and enemy of freedom; on the contrary, it alone can give and truly guarantee freedom. This fundamental conception was fixed for Rousseau from his first political writings on. The "Discours sur l'économie politique," which Rousseau wrote for the *Encyclopédie*, expresses it unmistakably. "It is to law alone that men owe justice and freedom; it is this [beneficial]

[27] [Friedrich Schiller, *Die Räuber*, Act I, Scene 2.]

58

organ of the will of all which reestablishes natural equality among men in the legal order; it is this celestial voice which prescribes to each citizen the precepts of public reason and teaches him to act in accord with the maxims of his own judgment, and not to be in contradiction with himself." [28]

On the other hand, this common dependence on the law is also the only legal ground for any social dependency whatever. A political community that demands any other kind of obedience is internally unsound. Freedom is destroyed when the community is asked to subject itself to the will of a single man or to a ruling group which can never be more than an association of individuals. The only "legitimate" authority is that authority which the principle of legitimacy, *the idea of law as such,* exercises over individual wills. At all times, this idea claims the individual only insofar as he is a member of the community, an actively participating organ of the general will, but not in his particular existence and individuality. No special privilege can be granted to an individual as individual or to a special class; no special effort can be demanded of him. In this sense the law must act "without respect of persons." A bond that does not bind absolutely everyone, but only this man or that, automatically nullifies itself. There can and must be no exceptions within the law nor by virtue of the law; rather, every exceptional decree to which single citizens or certain classes are subjected means by its very nature the destruction of the idea of law and of the state: the dissolution of the social contract and the relapse into the state of nature, which is characterized in this connection as a pure state of violence.[29]

In this sense it is the true fundamental task of the state to re-

[28] ["Economic politique" (Hachette ed., III, 283). This article, which originally appeared in Diderot's *Encyclopédie,* is also known as "Discours sur l'économie politique."]

[29] *Contrat social,* Livre II, Chap. iv [Hachette ed., III, 321–23].

place physical inequality among men, which is irremovable, with legal and moral equality.[30] Physical inequality is unavoidable, and it ought not to be deplored. In this category Rousseau includes the inequality of property, which in itself—merely as the unequal distribution of possessions—is of minor and subordinate importance in his thought. Truly communistic ideas are not developed anywhere in the *Contrat social*. For Rousseau, inequality of property is an *adiaphoron* [a matter of no moral significance], a fact which man can accept as much as he must put up with the unequal distribution of bodily strength, skills, and mental gifts. Here ends the realm of freedom, and the realm of fate begins.

Rousseau never conceived of the state as a mere welfare state. Unlike Diderot and the majority of the Encyclopedists, he did not regard it as merely the distributor of happiness. It does not guarantee to each individual an equal share of possessions; it is exclusively concerned with securing an equal measure of rights and duties. The state is therefore entitled and qualified to interfere with property insofar as the inequality of property endangers the moral equality of the subjects under the law—for instance, when such inequality condemns specific classes of citizens to complete economic dependence and threatens to make them a plaything in the hands of the wealthy and the powerful. In such a situation, the state may and must interfere. Through appropriate legislation, as for example through certain limitations on the right to inheritance, it must attempt to establish an equilibrium of economic forces. Rousseau's demands did not go beyond this.

It is true, however, that Rousseau regarded it as the proper characteristic of society—its original stigma, as it were—that it had always employed economic inequality to establish its rule of force and the harshest political tyranny. Rousseau fully appro-

[30] *Ibid.*, Livre I, Chap. ix [Hachette ed., III, 317–18].

priated Thomas More's pointed phrase that what had hitherto been called "state" had been nothing but a conspiracy of the rich against the poor. "You have need of me," says the rich man to the poor, "because I am rich and you are poor. Let us therefore make an agreement: I shall grant you the honor of serving me, on condition that you will give me the little you have left in return for the trouble I shall take to command you." [31]

Rousseau did not rebel against poverty as such. Rather, he fought with mounting bitterness the political and moral disfranchisement which is its inescapable consequence in the contemporary social order. "Are not all the advantages of society with the powerful and the rich? Are not all the lucrative posts filled with them alone? Are not all the favors, all the exemptions reserved for them? And is not the public authority in their favor? When an important man robs his creditors or commits other rascalities, is he not always sure of impunity? The beatings he deals out, the acts of violence he commits, even the killings and murders of which he becomes guilty—are these not matters that are hushed up and that are forgotten after six months? But if this same man is robbed, the whole police is set in motion immediately, and woe to the innocent whom he suspects! If he passes through a dangerous place, the escorts are out in force; if the axle of his post chaise breaks, everyone flies to his assistance. [. . .] If a cart finds itself in his way, his men are ready to beat the driver to death, and it is better if fifty honest pedestrians going about their business are crushed than that an idle scoundrel should be delayed in his carriage. All these attentions cost him not a penny—they are the rich man's right, and not the price of wealth." [32]

[31] ["Economie politique" (Hachette ed., III, 301).]
[32] "Discours sur l'économie politique," in Œuvres, Zweibrücken [Deux-Ponts], 1782, I, 237ff. [Hachette ed., III, 300].

Rousseau himself had experienced all the bitterness of poverty, but he was always armed with stoic equanimity against all physical deprivations. On the other hand, he never learned to endure the dependence of the will on the orders and arbitrariness of others. This is the starting point both for his ideal of the state as well as for his ideal of education. The fundamental idea of *Emile* consists in this: that no physical obstacles must be removed from the path of the pupil who is to be educated to independence of will and character. He is to be spared no suffering, no effort, no privation, and he is to be anxiously protected only from violent coercion by an outside will, from a command whose necessity he does not understand. He is to become acquainted with the compulsion of things from his earliest childhood, and he is to learn to bow before it; but he is to be spared the tyranny of men.

The tendency of Rousseau's political and social theory can be fully understood only from the perspective of this fundamental idea: its essential purpose, it is true, is to place the individual under a law that is universally binding, but this law is to be shaped in such a manner that every shadow of caprice and arbitrariness disappears from it. We should learn to submit to the law of the community just as we submit to the law of nature; we are not to acquiesce in it as in an alien dictate but must follow it because we recognize its necessity. This is possible when—and only when—we understand that this law is of such a nature that we must assent to it freely when we assimilate its meaning and can absorb this meaning into our own will.

With this conception, the state is faced with a new demand and challenge which has rarely been sounded so sharply and firmly since the days of Plato. For its essential task, the point of departure and the basis of all government, is the task of education. The state does not simply address itself to already existing and given subjects of the will; rather its first aim is to *create* the sort of subjects to whom it can address its call. Unless the will is thus formed, mastery over the will must always be illusory and futile.

The objection has frequently been raised against the social-contract theory in general and against Rousseau's *Contrat social* in particular that it is an atomistic-mechanistic theory, that it views the state's universal will as a mere aggregate composed of the wills of all individuals. But this reproach mistakes the essence of Rousseau's fundamental intention. From the formal point of view, it is true, Rousseau had a good deal of difficulty in delimiting, clearly and firmly, the *volonté générale* against the *volonté de tous,* and in the *Contrat social* we can find not a few passages that would seem to indicate that the content of the general will could be determined purely quantitatively, by the simple counting of individual votes. No doubt, there are flaws of exposition, but these flaws do not touch the core of Rousseau's fundamental thought.

Indeed, Rousseau did not by any means regard the state as a mere "association," as a community of interests and an equilibrium of the interests of individual wills. According to him, it is not a mere empirical collection of certain dispositions, impulses, and vacillating appetites, but the form in which the will, as ethical will, really exists. In that state alone can willfulness develop into will. Law in its pure and strict sense is not a mere external bond that holds in individual wills and prevents their scattering; rather it is the constituent principle of these wills, the element that confirms and justifies them spiritually. It wishes to rule subjects only inasmuch as, in its every act, it also makes and educates them into citizens.

This ideal task, not the happiness and welfare of the individual, is the real purpose of the state. But to comprehend this task in its essence, men must raise themselves above all hitherto existing empirical-historical forms of political communities. Neither a comparison of these forms nor their conceptual articulation and classification—as was attempted by Montesquieu in his *Esprit des lois*—can yield the real justification of the state. Rousseau explicitly objected to such an empirical, abstract method. "At first glance all human institutions seem to be founded on heaps of quicksand. It is only when we examine them closely, only when we have cleared away the dust and sand that surround the edifice, that we begin to see the firm foundation on which it is erected and that we learn to respect its basis." [33] Instead of shaping the state freely and building within it the order appropriate to men, mankind had, up to then, been the property of the state. Need had driven man to the state and had held him there—long before he was able to understand and inwardly to comprehend its necessity.

But now at last this hold had to be broken. The state created by mere necessity was to become the state created by reason. Just as Bacon had called for the *regnum hominis* over nature, so Rousseau now made the same demand for the proper spheres of man—state and society. So long as these were left to merely physical wants and to the rule of emotions and passions, so long as they were made into the proving grounds of the instinct of power and domination, ambition and self-love, any additional strengthening of the state only created a new scourge for man. Society up to then had burdened man with innumerable evils and had entangled him ever more deeply in error and vice. But man is not subject to this entanglement as to an inescapable fate. He can and he ought to free himself from it by taking the control of his destiny into his own hands, by substituting "I will" and "I should" for a mere "I must." It is the business of man, and it is within his power, to transform into a blessing the curse which had up to then lain over all political and social developments. But he can accomplish this task only after he has found and understood himself.

[33] *Discours sur l'inégalité*, Préface [Hachette ed., I, 82].

Rousseau's *Contrat social* wraps both demands into one. State and society are to find each other in mutual interaction; they are to grow and unfold together, so as to become inextricably joined in this common growth. What Rousseau now recognized was that man as such is neither good nor evil, neither happy nor unhappy; for his essence and his form are not rigid data but are malleable. And the most important, the essentially plastic power Rousseau saw contained in the community. He now realized that the new humanity for which he yearned must remain a dream so long as the state was not radically transformed.

In this manner the *Discours sur l'inégalité* and the *Contrat social*, in spite of all apparent contradictions interlock and complement each other. They contradict each other so little that each can rather be explained only through and with the other. If we regard the *Contrat social* as a foreign body in Rousseau's writings, we have failed to understand the spiritual organism of his work. Throughout, Rousseau's entire interest and passion were given to the doctrine of man. But he had come to understand that the question, What is man? cannot be separated from the question, What ought he to be?

Once, in the *Confessions,* he unambiguously described his inner development in that sense: "I had realized that everything was basically related to politics, and that, no matter how one approached it, no people would ever be anything but what the nature of its government made it. Therefore that great question of the best possible government seemed to me to reduce itself to this: which is the form of government fitted to shape the most virtuous, the most enlightened, the wisest, and, in short, the 'best' people, taking that word in its noblest meaning?" [34] And this question leads us back to the other and separate question: Which is the form of government that most completely realizes

[34] *Confessions,* Livre IX (near the beginning) [Hachette ed., VIII, 288–89].

within itself, by virtue of its nature, the pure rule of law?[35]

It was by assigning this ethical task to politics, by subordinating politics to this ethical imperative, that Rousseau accomplished his truly revolutionary act. With that act he stood alone in his century. He was by no means the first nor the only man to have felt the grave political and social ills of his time and to have expressed himself on them openly. In the midst of the splendid era of Louis XIV these ills had been recognized and characterized keenly by the noblest and profoundest minds of the age. Fénelon had taken the lead; others, such as Vauban, Boulainvilliers, and Boisguillebert, had followed him.[36] In the eighteenth century Montesquieu, Turgot, D'Argenson, Voltaire, Diderot, and Holbach joined and continued this movement. Everywhere, a genuine and strong will to reform was at work; everywhere, the most unsparing criticism was exercised on the Old Regime. And yet this will to reform neither explicitly nor implicitly rose to revolutionary demands. The thinkers of the Encyclopedist circle wanted to ameliorate and to cure; but hardly one of them believed in the necessity for, or in the possibility of, a radical transformation and reformation of state and society. They were satisfied when they succeeded in eliminating the worst abuses and in leading mankind gradually into better political conditions.

All these thinkers were convinced eudaemonists; they sought the happiness of men, and they agreed that this happiness could be truly promoted and secured only through slow, stubborn labor, in single, groping experiments. They expected that the progress of insight and intellectual cultivation would lead to new forms of communal life, but they professed to see that this progress was always reserved to the few, and that the impulse for im-

[35] [Cf.] *Contrat social,* Livre II, Chap. vi [Hachette ed., III, 325–36].

[36] On this point, cf. the collection of texts by Henri Sée, *Les Idées politiques en France au XVIIe siècle* (Paris, 1923).

provement could therefore come only from them. Thus, with all their demands for freedom, they became advocates of "enlightened despotism."

Voltaire was not content with the theoretical proclamation and justification of his political and social ideals. He himself lent a hand, and in the last decades of his life he had a most extensive and beneficent impact. He paved the way for a number of highly important reforms through his personal intercession and by taking advantage of his European reputation. He spoke up for freedom of the person, for the abolition of slavery and serfdom, for freedom of conscience and of the press, for the freedom of work, for fundamental reforms within the penal code, and for decisive improvements in the tax system.[37] But he did not demand a radical political renewal and he did not believe in a radical ethical renewal. All such thoughts and desires he regarded as dreams and Utopias, which he brushed aside with sarcasm. He professed to know and to see that all such chimeras make men neither better nor wiser but merely entangle them ever more deeply in error and guilt:

> Nous tromper dans nos entreprises,
> C'est à quoi nous sommes sujets.
> Le matin je fais des projets,
> Et le long du jour des sottises.[38]

These are the words with which Voltaire introduces his philosophical satire, *Memnon, ou La Sagesse humaine* (1747). It describes the fate of a man who one day resolves to become completely wise —to surrender to no passion, to renounce all the pleasures of life,

[37] For details, see G[ustave] Lanson, *Voltaire* (Paris: Hachette, 6th ed.), p. 180.

[38] [*Œuvres,* ed. M. Beuchot (Paris: Lefèvre, 1834-40), XXXIII, 152.

> To turn out wrong is, as a rule,
> The fate of human enterprise.
> I form great projects as I rise
> And all day long act like a fool.]

67

and to be guided entirely by reason. The outcome of this resolution is pitiful: Memnon ends up in misery and disgrace. A good spirit appears to him and promises him salvation, but only on condition that he will renounce once and for all his foolish intention to become completely wise. Such was the fundamental disposition to which Voltaire held fast in his literary and philosophical work. For him the wise man was not the one who liberates himself from all human weaknesses and shortcomings but the man who sees through them and uses them to guide humanity. " 'Tis folly to wait for fools to grow wise! Children of wisdom, make fools out of fools, as indeed they deserve." [39]

The next generation, the younger Encyclopedists, went beyond Voltaire's political ideas and demands. Diderot did not remain within the horizon of ideas of enlightened despotism; he developed pronounced democratic ideas and ideals, and he was naive enough to submit them to his patroness, Catherine II of Russia, who brushed them aside as absurd.[40] But he too was content with details; he too believed that the political and social world could not be saved by a drastic cure. This political opportunism marked the true spirit of the *Encyclopédie*. Holbach, who in respect to religion and metaphysics pursued radical logic to its extreme limits and who advanced to a consistent atheism, was no exception here. "No," he exclaims in the draft of his social system, "not through dangerous convulsions, not through struggle, through regicides and useless crime, can the wounds of the nations be healed. These violent remedies are always more cruel than the evils they are in-

[39] [Goethe, "Kophtisches Lied," in *Gesellige Lieder*:
        Töricht! auf Bessrung der Toren zu harren!
        Kinder der Klugheit, o habet die Narren
        Eben zum Narren auch, wie sich's gehört.]

[40] On Diderot's political theory and his relations with Catherine II, cf. Morley, *Diderot and the Encyclopaedists* (1878; new ed., London, 1923), II, 90ff. See also Henri Sée, *Les Idées politiques en France au XVIIIe siècle* (Paris, 1920), pp. 137ff.

tended to cure. [. . .] The voice of reason is neither seditious nor bloodthirsty. The reforms which it proposes may be slow, but therefore planned all the better." [41] It was this circumspection, this prudence, this shrewd and cautious weighing of all circumstances that the whole Encyclopedic circle felt lacking in Rousseau's political and social system.[42] D'Alembert, who embodied all the ideals of this circle, a mathematician of genius and an independent philosophical thinker, made this very demand the center of his critique of Rousseau's *Emile:* It is futile to rave against evils; men must seek cures for them, and the cures that philosophy can suggest can be nothing but palliatives. "We can no longer conquer the enemy; he has advanced too far into the land for us to attempt to drive him out; our task is reduced to waging guerrilla warfare against him." [43]

But Rousseau's personality and mentality did not dispose him to such guerrilla warfare, such a *guerre de chicane,* as D'Alembert called it, nor would he have been able to wage it. He was no more of an active revolutionary than the Encyclopedists were; direct intervention in politics was always far from his mind. Rousseau, the outcast and the eccentric, shied away from the turmoil of the market place and the noise of battle. And yet the truly revolutionary impetus emanated from him, not from the men who represented and dominated the public state of mind of contemporary France. He did not concern himself with single evils, nor did he seek single cures. For him there was no compromise with existing society, no attempt at alleviating mere superficial symptoms. He rejected all partial solutions; first and last, and with

[41] Holbach, *Système social,* [Partie] II, [Chap.] ii [(Paris: Niogret, 1822), p. 345].

[42] On the relation of Rousseau's political theory to the political theories of the Encyclopedists, cf. the excellent treatment by R[ené] Hubert, *Les Sciences sociales dans l'Encyclopédie* (Paris, 1923).

[43] D'Alembert, "Jugement d'Emile" in *Œuvres* (Paris: Didier, 1853), pp. 295ff.

every word he wrote, it was all or nothing with him. For he saw in the state neither the creator and preserver of happiness nor the guardian and increaser of power. To the ideas of the welfare state and the power state he opposed the idea of the constitutional state (*Rechtsstaat*). For Rousseau this was not a matter of more or less, but of either/or.

Radicalism of this sort is possible only to a thinker who is more than a mere thinker, a man who is not exclusively dominated by cerebration but who is driven onward by an ethical imperative. This is why the only absolute ethical thinker that the eighteenth century produced, the champion of the "primacy of the practical reason," was almost alone in understanding Rousseau completely on this point. When Kant writes that there is no value to human existence on this earth if justice is not brought to triumph, he expresses a genuinely Rousseauist thought and sentiment. Rousseau himself, it is true, was unable to break theoretically the hold of the eudaemonism which dominated all eighteenth-century ethics. From the outset, his whole thought was moved by the problem of happiness: its aim was to find a harmonious union of virtue and happiness.

Here Rousseau called upon religion for help; he clung to the belief in immortality, which to him seemed the only possible way of bringing about and guaranteeing the ultimate union of "being happy" (*Glückseligkeit*) and "deserving to be happy" (*Glückwürdigkeit*). "Toutes les subtilités de la Métaphysique," he wrote to Voltaire, "ne me feront pas douter un moment de l'immortalité de l'âme et d'une Providence bienfaisante. Je le sens, je le crois, je le veux, je l'espère, je le défendrai jusqu'à mon dernier soupir." [44] And yet we would be mistaken if—as has been done in

[44] To Voltaire, August 18, 1756 [Hachette ed., X, 133]. ["All the subtleties of metaphysics will not make me doubt for a moment the immortality of the soul or a beneficent Providence. I feel it, I believe it, I want it, I hope for it, and I shall defend it to my last breath."]

the most recent comprehensive account of Rousseau's thought [45] —we sought to make this point the center and core of his doctrine, and if we regarded this doctrine as the answer to the question, How can happiness and virtue be reconciled in human existence? For even when speaking the language of eudaemonism, Rousseau in his inner being transcended this formulation of the problem. His ethical and political ideal does not pursue, as does that of Voltaire and Diderot, purely utilitarian goals. He did not inquire into happiness or utility; he was concerned with the dignity of man and with the means of securing and realizing it.

Rousseau never paid special attention to the problem of physical evil; he faced it almost with indifference. The only way of meeting it—this is the fundamental thought which he makes the center of his educational plan in *Emile*—is to despise it and to learn to inure oneself to it. But this solution had no validity for social evil. This could not be borne because it ought not to be borne; because it robs man not of his happiness but of his essence and his destiny. At this point no retreat, no pliancy or submissiveness is permitted. What Voltaire, D'Alembert, Diderot, regarded as mere defects of society, as mere mistakes in organization which must be gradually eliminated, Rousseau saw rather as the guilt of society, and with flaming words, again and again, he reproached society with this guilt and called for atonement. He rejected the arguments of bare need and inescapable necessity; he denied all appeals to the experience of centuries. The verdict of the past had no validity for him because he had fixed his eyes imperturbably on the future and had assigned to society the task of bringing into being a new future for mankind.

And with this we stand before a new problem which will take us a step closer in our approach to the true center of Rousseau's world of ideas. Kant, in a well-known pronouncement, credited

[45] Cf. Schinz, *La Pensée de Jean-Jacques Rousseau* (Paris, 1929).

Rousseau with no less an achievement than the solution of the theodicy problem and placed him, for this reason, beside Newton. "Newton was the first to see order and regularity combined with great simplicity, where disorder and ill-matched variety had reigned before. Since then comets have been moving in geometric orbits. Rousseau was the first to discover in the variety of shapes that men assume the deeply concealed nature of man and to observe the hidden law that justifies Providence. Before them, the objections of Alfonso and Manes still had validity. After Newton and Rousseau, God is justified, and from now on Pope's maxim is true." [46]

These sentences are strange, and difficult to interpret. What are those "observations" of Rousseau's which justify the ways of God? What new principles concerning the problem of theodicy did Rousseau add to the thought of Leibniz, of Shaftesbury, of Pope? Does not everything he said on this problem move in familiar paths, known to the whole eighteenth century? And in any event, is it not part of that dogmatic metaphysics whose fundamental form Kant himself had done away with and which he later exposed with all its defects in a special essay, "Über das Misslingen aller philosophischen Versuche in der Theodizee"? [47] And yet Kant, even as the critic of pure and practical reason, never wavered in this estimate of Rousseau. He saw through the surface of the metaphysical chain of proof. He comprehended the core of Rousseau's fundamental ethical and religious outlook, and in that outlook he recognized his own. Rousseau's *Emile,* which, as we

[46] Kant, *Werke* (Hartenstein), VIII, 630. [Cf. Leibniz, *Theodicy,* Part Two, Par. 193: "There are people who hold that God could have done it better. This is practically the error of the well-known Alfonso, king of Castile who was elected king of Rome by several electors, and who promoted the astronomical tables that are named after him. This king is supposed to have said that if God had consulted him when He created the world, he could have given Him good advice."]

[47] [In 1791. Kant, *Werke,* ed. by Ernst Cassirer (Berlin: B. Cassirer, 1912-22), VI, 119-38.]

know, was among Kant's favorite books, begins with the statement, "Tout est bien en sortant des mains de l'Auteur des choses; tout dégénère entre les mains de l'homme." [48] Thus God seems relieved of responsibility, and blame for all evil is ascribed to man.

This, however, presents us with a difficult problem and an apparently insoluble contradiction. For was it not precisely Rousseau who again and again proclaimed the doctrine of the original goodness of human nature, and who made this very doctrine the center and pivot of all his thought? How can evil and guilt be attributed to human nature if it is free from both in its original state, if it knows no radical depravity? This is the question around which Rousseau's thought circled ever anew.

For us, theodicy is a historical problem. We no longer consider it a current question that immediately concerns and presses us. But in the seventeenth and eighteenth centuries the preoccupation with this question was by no means a mere conceptual and dialectical game. The profoundest spirits of that epoch constantly wrestled with it and regarded it as the truly vital question of ethics and religion. Rousseau, too, found himself inwardly bound to and rooted in religion because of this problem. He took up the old battle for the justification of God against the philosophy of the century, and as a result he quarreled with the Encyclopedist movement, with Holbach and his circle.

He was to find out, however, that he, who considered himself a genuine "defender of the faith" on this point, was to be most implacably opposed, persecuted, and even excommunicated by the official guardians of that faith. It was one of the tragic misunderstandings of Rousseau's life that he never understood the significance of this struggle, that he never saw anything but violence

[48] [Hachette ed., II, 3. "All is good as it leaves the hands of the Author of things, all degenerates in the hands of men."]

and arbitrariness in the persecution directed against him. Yet, from a purely historical point of view, this judgment was unjust to the Church and, in a certain sense, to himself. In fact, an inescapable decision, vital to the history of the world and to cultural history, was involved. What irrevocably separated Rousseau, despite all his genuine and deep religious emotion, from all traditional forms of faith was the decisiveness with which he rejected every thought of the *original* sin of man.

No understanding or reconciliation was possible here: in the seventeenth and eighteenth centuries the dogma of original sin stood in the center and focus of Catholic and Protestant theology. All great religious movements of the time were oriented toward and gathered up in this dogma. The struggles over Jansenism in France; the battles between Gomarists and Arminians in Holland; the development of Puritanism in England and of Pietism in Germany—they all stood under this sign. And now this fundamental conviction concerning the radical evil in human nature was to find in Rousseau a dangerous and uncompromising adversary.

The Church fully understood this situation: it stressed, at once, the decisive issue with full clarity and firmness. The mandate in which Christophe de Beaumont, archbishop of Paris, condemns *Emile,* laid the chief emphasis on Rousseau's denial of original sin. The claim that the first emotions of human nature are always innocent and good, he asserted, stands in sharpest contradiction to all the teachings of Holy Writ and of the Church concerning the essence of man.[49]

Rousseau now seemed to have placed himself in a completely untenable position: on the one hand he upheld—against the Church—the original goodness of human nature and the right and

[49] Cf. "Mandement de Monseigneur l'Archevêque de Paris, portant condamnation d'un livre qui a pour titre *Emile"* ([Rousseau], *Œuvres,* éd. Zweibrücken [Deux-Ponts], Suppléments, V, 262ff.) [Hachette ed., III, 45–57].

independence of human reason; on the other hand, he repudiated the noblest achievements of this reason—art, science, and all spiritual cultivation. Could he still legitimately complain of his complete isolation, an isolation which he himself had created by estranging himself from the dominant forms of faith as well as by quarreling with the philosophical Enlightenment? In addition to this external isolation, he now seemed torn by an insoluble inner dilemma. The obscurity of the theodicy problem henceforth seemed completely impenetrable. For if we can neither trace evil back to God nor find its cause in the character of human nature, where are we to find its source and origin?

Rousseau's solution of this dilemma lies in his placing responsibility at a point where no one before him had looked for it. He created, as it were, a new subject of responsibility, of "imputability." This subject is not individual man, but human society. The individual as such, as he emerges from the hands of nature, is not yet involved in the antithesis of good and evil: he gives himself up to his natural instinct of self-preservation. He is governed by *amour de soi;* but this self-love never degenerates into "selfish love" (*amour propre*), whose only satisfying pleasure is the oppression of others. Selfish love, which contains the cause of all future depravity and fosters man's vanity and thirst for power, is exclusively to be charged to society. It is selfish love that makes man a tyrant over nature and over himself; awakens in him needs and passions which the natural man had not known; and at the same time places into his hands ever new means for achieving the unfettered and ruthless gratification of these desires. Our eagerness to be talked about, our furious ambition to distinguish ourselves before others—all this keeps us constantly from ourselves and throws us, as it were, outside ourselves.[50]

[50] *Discours sur l'inégalité* (*Œuvres*, Zweibrücken [Deux-Ponts], pp. 75ff., 90ff., 138ff., and elsewhere) [Hachette ed., I, 71–152 *passim*].

But is this alienation of the essence of *every* society? Can we not imagine a development toward a genuine and truly human community which will no longer require these springs of power, greed, and vanity but will be rooted wholly in common subjection to a law that is inwardly recognized as binding and necessary? Should such a community arise and endure, evil, as social evil (and this, as we have seen, alone counts in Rousseau's considerations), will be overcome and removed. The hour of salvation will strike when the present coercive form of society is destroyed and is replaced by the free form of political and ethical community—a community in which everyone obeys only the general will, which he recognizes and acknowledges as his own will, rather than be subjected to the willfulness of others. But it is futile to hope that this salvation will be accomplished through outside help. No God can grant it to us; man must become his own savior and, in the ethical sense, his own creator. In its present form society has inflicted the deepest wounds on humanity; but society alone can and should heal these wounds. The burden of responsibility rests upon it from now on.

That is Rousseau's solution of the problem of theodicy—and with it he had indeed placed the problem on completely new ground. He had carried it beyond the realm of metaphysics and placed it in the center of ethics and politics. With this act he gave it a stimulus which continues to work unabated even today. All contemporary social struggles are still moved and driven by this original stimulus. They are rooted in that consciousness of the *responsibility* of society which Rousseau was the first to possess and which he implanted in all posterity.

The seventeenth century had not yet known this idea. When that century was at its height, Bossuet once more proclaimed the old theocratic ideal and established it in its unconditionality and absoluteness. The state coincides with the ruler, and the ruler is subject to no human power or human control; he is responsible to God alone and can be called to account only by him. In opposition to this theocratic absolutism there arose the resolute resistance of the natural law of the seventeenth and eighteenth centuries. Natural law is not a divine but a specifically human law, and it is equally binding on all human wills, rulers as well as ruled. But even this declaration of original, inalienable "rights of man" did not immediately destroy the form of the coercive state, though it limited its powers. In the *Contrat social* Rousseau still carried on a running argument with Grotius, because the latter had admitted at least the possibility of the legality of slavery. Grotius had argued that slavery could possibly be justified by the original contract from which society had arisen. The conqueror of a country, for example, might have concluded a contract with the vanquished that would assure them their lives under the condition that they surrender themselves and their descendants to the victor as his property. Rousseau, in contrast, angrily pushed aside all these reservations as mere formal juristic constructions. Against them he insisted on the "right with which we are born"—and he believed that this right is violated by slavery in any form. If we say that the son of a slave is born a slave, that means no less than that he is not born a man.[51] The true, legitimate society can never honor such a claim; for it is nothing if not the guardian of that *volonté générale,* to which there are no exceptions and from which no one can escape.

Rousseau's solution of the theodicy problem, then, consisted in his removing the burden of responsibility from God and putting it on human society. If society cannot shoulder this burden, if it fails to accomplish, in free responsibility, what its self-determination demands of it, it is guilty. It has been pointed out, and

[51] *Contrat social,* Livre IV, Chap. ii, and esp. Livre I, Chap. iv. [Hachette ed., III, 368, 309–12].

rightly so, that there are quite definite formal analogies between Rousseau's doctrine of the "state of nature" and the Christian doctrine of the state of innocence. Rousseau, too, knew an expulsion of men from the paradise of innocence; he, too, saw in man's development into a rational animal a kind of "fall from grace" that excludes man forever from the secure and well-protected happiness that he had enjoyed up to then. But if, in this respect, Rousseau deplored the gift of "perfectibility" which differentiates man from all other living creatures,[52] he also knew that it alone can bring ultimate deliverance. It is only through this gift, not through divine aid and salvation, that man will finally reap freedom and master his fate: "Car l'impulsion du seul appétit est l'esclavage et l'obéissance à la loi qu'on s'est prescrite est liberté."[53]

It is only in this context that the controversial problem of Rousseau's "optimism" is placed in its proper light. At first glance it seems strange that this brooding and melancholy hermit, this disappointed man whose life ended in complete darkness and isolation, should cling to the thesis of optimism to the end of his life and become one of its most zealous champions. In his correspondence with Voltaire, Rousseau had not failed to point out the tragic paradox that he, the stepchild of fortune, the hunted and the outcast of society, should take up the defense of optimism against Voltaire, who was living in the splendor of fame and in the enjoyment of all worldly goods. But this paradox disappears when we observe that Rousseau and Voltaire understood the problem of optimism in two completely different senses. For Voltaire, this was fundamentally not a question of philosophy but purely a question of temperament and mood. In the first decades of his

[52] Cf. *Discours sur l'inégalité*, Première Partie [Hachette ed., I, 90].

[53] *Contrat social*, Livre I, Chap. viii [Hachette ed., III, 316]. ["For the impulse of mere appetite is slavery, and the obedience to the law which we have prescribed to ourselves is liberty."]

life he did not only indulge without restraint in all the enjoyments of life but made himself their advocate and glorifier. In the midst of the deep decadence and depravity of the age of the Regency he became the apologist of the era. His philosophical poem *Le Mondain* sings the praise of his age:

> Moi je rends grâce à la nature sage
> Qui, pour mon bien, m'a fait naître en cet âge
> Tant décrié par nos tristes frondeurs;
> Ce temps profane est tout fait pour mes mœurs.
> J'aime le luxe, et méme la mollesse,
> Tous les plaisirs, les arts de toute espèce,
> La propreté, le goût, les ornements;
> Tout honnête homme a de tels sentiments.
>
> .   .   .   .
>
> L'or de la terre et les trésors de l'onde
> Leurs habitants et les peuples de l'air
> Tout sert au luxe, aux plaisirs de ce monde,
> O le bon temps que ce siècle de fer! [54]

It would seem that Voltaire later regretted this glorification. The earthquake of Lisbon frightened him out of his calm and complacency and he nearly became a moral preacher against a generation that could skip lightheartedly over even such horrors:

[54] Voltaire, *Le Mondain* (1736), in *Œuvres* (Paris: Lequin, 1825), XIV, 112.
> [I say, let kindly nature e'er be praised,
> Who in her wisdom caused me to be raised
> In this our age which malcontents revile:
> These worldly times exactly suit my style.
> I'm fond of luxury and even of soft ease,
> I love all pleasures, all the arts that please,
> Cleanliness, taste, and ornaments refined:
> On this, all decent men are of my mind.
>
> .   .   .   .
>
> All the gold of the earth and all the ocean's treasures,
> The creatures of the land, the air, the sea,
> All serve to heighten luxury and pleasures—
> Oh iron age, what bliss to live in thee!]

Lisbonne, qui n'est plus, eut-elle plus de vices
Que Londres, que Paris plongés dans les délices?
Lisbonne est abîmée et l'on danse à Paris!

Explicitly Voltaire now opposed the earlier hymn of praise with this ode of retraction:

Sur un ton moins lugubre on me vit autrefois
Chanter des doux plaisirs les séduisantes lois:
D'autres temps, d'autres mœurs: instruit par la vieillesse
Des humains égarés partageant la faiblesse
Sous une épaisse nuit cherchant à m'éclairer
Je ne sais que souffrir, et non pas murmurer.[55]

Unwilling to grumble against the sufferings of the world, he would rather exercise his wit at the expense of the "system" of optimism, over which he pours all the vials of his scorn in *Candide*. In this work his satirical mood found ever bitterer expression, but this bitterness was far removed from embitterment. Fundamentally, Voltaire's attitude toward life had remained almost unchanged since his youth. Now as before he combined the sharpest skepticism with a decisive affirmation of the world and of life.

These two moods emerge most clearly in the philosophical tale *Le Monde comme il va, Vision de Babouc* (1746).[56] Ituriel, an angel of the highest rank, orders Babouc to go to the capital of

---

[55] *Poème sur le désastre de Lisbonne* (1756), in *Œuvres*, XII, 186.

> [Had Lisbon, now destroyed, more vices to repent
> Than London or than Paris, still on pleasure bent?
> Yet Lisbon's ruins smoke while Paris dances.
>
> .   .   .   .   .
>
> I praised you once, in less lugubrious measures,
> Seductive laws that guide our gentle pleasures.
> Time changes customs; age has taught my mind.
> Weak like the rest of wayward humankind,
> I seek the light of truth in darkest night
> And without murmuring accept my plight.]

[56] [*Œuvres*, ed. by M. Beuchot, XXXIII, 1–26.]

the Persian Empire to observe the activities of men and the customs of the city. On his report and verdict depends the survival or destruction of Persepolis. He becomes thoroughly acquainted with the city. He observes its unbridled excesses; he learns of the abuse and insolence of office, the venality of judges, the fraudulent machinations of commerce. But at the same time he sees the city in its glory, in its magnificence, its spiritual and sociable civilization. And thus he makes up his mind. He has a small statue made by the most skillful goldsmith in the city—made up of all metals, the most precious and the basest—and brings it to Ituriel. "Would you break this pretty statue," he asks the angel, "because it does not consist wholly of gold and diamonds?" Ituriel understands: "Il résolut de ne pas même songer à corriger Persépolis, et de laisser aller *le monde comme il va;* car, dit-il, si tout n'est pas bien, tout est passable." [57]

This was Voltaire's last word on the world and on worldly life. Even his pessimism remained playful, while Rousseau's optimism was filled with and sustained by tragic seriousness. For even when Rousseau painted the bliss of the senses and of the sensual passions in the most glowing colors, he was not satisfied with this picture alone, but placed it against a dark and gloomy background. He did not believe in the unrestrained surrender to passion but demanded of men the power of renunciation. The meaning and worth of life disclosed themselves to him only in that power. Rousseau's optimism is the heroic optimism of Plutarch, his favorite author, and of the great models of ancient history, to whom Rousseau liked to turn for inspiration. He demanded that men, instead of losing themselves in idle laments over the miseries of existence, should understand their destiny and master it themselves. All his political and social ideals grew

[57] ["He decided not even to dream of correcting Persepolis, and to let the world go its own way; for, he said, if all is not well, at least all is passable."]

out of this demand. Rousseau himself reports in his *Confessions* that while he was occupied in the composition of the *Discours sur l'inégalité* he was constantly driven by the urge to call out to men: "Fools, who endlessly complain about nature, learn that all your troubles come from yourselves!" [58]

In this manner this supposed "irrationalist" ended up with the most resolute belief in reason. For Rousseau, the belief in the victory of reason coincided with his belief in the victory of the genuine "cosmopolitan constitution." This belief, too, he communicated to Kant. Kant displays a Rousseauist outlook and mentality when he describes as mankind's greatest problem the establishment of a society of citizens which administers law universally, and when he regards the history of mankind in general as the fulfillment of a hidden plan of nature, designed to achieve an internally and, for this purpose, externally perfect constitution. The theodicy problem can be solved only in and through the state. It is man's business and it is his loftiest task to accomplish the justification of God—not by means of metaphysical broodings over happiness and unhappiness and over good and evil but by freely creating and freely shaping the order in accordance with which he wants to live.

[58] *Confessions*, Livre VIII [Hachette ed., VIII, 277].

2

IF WE SEEK TO UNDERSTAND Rousseau's accomplishment in its historic significance, if we seek to characterize it by its immediate effect, it would seem that we could compress this effect into one point. The specifically and characteristically new contribution that Rousseau made to his time seems to have been his act of freeing it from the domination of intellectualism. To the forces of rationalist understanding, on which rested the culture of the eighteenth century, he opposed the force of feeling. Challenging the power of reflective and analytical reason, he became the discoverer of passion and of its irresistible primitive force. It was, in fact, a completely new current of life that penetrated into French spirituality and threatened to dissolve all its established forms and to flood its carefully erected dikes.

Up to then, neither the philosophy nor the poetry of eighteenth-century France had been touched by this current. For even poetry had long since forgotten to speak the elemental language of feeling and passion. Classical tragedy had been frozen in its pattern; the heroic impulse from which it had originally sprung had lost its power. Henceforth, tragedy merely repeated outmoded themes; its genuine and strong pathos ebbed and finally dissolved in mere rhetoric. With Voltaire's dramas, tragedy became enslaved to analysis and dialectic. Voltaire himself, who unceasingly strove for the laurels of the tragic poet, was too keen an observer and critic to be able to conceal from himself this retrogression and

83

decadence. In the *Siècle de Louis XIV* he admitted with resignation that the classic epoch of the drama was over—that only imitation but no fundamental feelings could exist in this area. "Il ne faut pas croire que les grandes passions tragiques et les grands sentiments puissent se varier à l'infini d'une manière neuve et frappante. Tout a ses bornes. . . . Le génie n'a qu'un siècle, après quoi il faut qu'il dégénère." [1]

This torpor was even more strikingly apparent in the field of lyric poetry. Before the advent of Rousseau spontaneous lyrical sentiment seemed to have almost completely dried up in France. The very name and genre of the lyrical species seemed completely forgotten by French aesthetics. Boileau's *Art poétique* had carefully sought to classify all single species of poetry—tragedy, comedy, fables, the didactic poem, the epigram—and to prescribe rules for each. But lyric poetry found no room in this classification and codification of poetic forms; no individual essential quality was ascribed to it. Aesthetics seemed to be drawing only the logical consequence from this development when it regarded poetic form more and more as a mere external ornament, an incidental appendage, which hinders rather than helps artistic truth and representation. With writers such as Fontenelle and La Motte-Houdar, aesthetics became a glorification of prose; it alone could supposedly reach the highest clarity of expression and ideas, because it avoided vagueness and metaphor in order to let the subject matter speak for itself in its simple "naturalness." To this standard of naturalness—that is, to intellectual clarity and definition—La Motte tried to reduce even Homer in his translation of the *Iliad*. Tragedy and the ode he also sought to lead back to prose form, in order thus to liberate them from their false en-

[1] Voltaire, *Siècle de Louis XIV*, Chap. xxxii. ["It must not be thought that the great tragic passions and the great sentiments can be infinitely varied in a new and striking manner. Everything has its limits. . . . Genius flourishes in only one century; after that it is bound to degenerate."]

thusiasm, from allegory and parable, from the *figures audacieuses*.

If, with all this, poetic species remained alive at all in the eighteenth century; if, indeed, verse acquired unprecedented agility and facility, this very facility sprang largely from the fact that poetry was no longer burdened with any properly poetic content. Verse had become a mere shell to which thought conformed. It served to clothe a philosophic and moral truth and was the convenient means for a didactic end. Thus, in the midst of an abundance and superabundance of poetic production, all living sources of poetry dried up; thus began that epoch in French literature which has been called "la poésie sans poésie." [2]

The spell that rested on French language and poetry was broken only by Rousseau. Without creating a single piece of what might properly be called lyrical poetry, he discovered and resurrected the world of lyricism. It was the revelation of this almost forgotten world in Rousseau's *Nouvelle Héloïse* that so deeply moved and so strongly shook his contemporaries. They saw in this novel no mere creation of the imagination. They felt transplanted from the sphere of literature into the core of a new existence and enriched with a new feeling for life. Rousseau was the first to perceive this *vita nuova* and the first to awaken it in others. In himself, this feeling had grown out of the direct communion with nature which he had cultivated from the first awakening of his spiritual self-awareness. He taught nature to speak once more, and he never forgot her language, which he had learned in his childhood and adolescence. He plunged into it and intoxicated himself with it long after he had become a solitary misanthrope who avoided all intercourse with men. "Recovered from the sweet myth of friendship," so he describes himself in the first dialogue of *Rousseau juge de Jean-Jacques*, "[. . .] finding among men neither integrity nor truth, nor any

[2] Cf. Gustave Lanson, *Histoire de la littérature française*, 5e partie, Chap. ii.

of the feelings [. . .] without which all society is but illusion and vanity, I withdrew into myself; and, in living with myself and with nature, I tasted an infinite sweetness in the thought that I was not alone, that I was not speaking to an unfeeling and dead being. [. . .] I have never adopted the philosophy of the happy men of this age; it was not made for me, I sought a philosophy more appropriate to the heart, more comforting in adversity, and more encouraging to virtue." [3]

Thus Rousseau's lyrical power, which he proved at its deepest and purest in the first part of the *Nouvelle Héloïse,* lay in his ability to depict all human sentiment and passion as if enveloped in the atmosphere of pure sensitivity to nature. Here man no longer simply stands "over against" nature—nature is not a drama which he enjoys as a mere spectator and observer; he dips into its inner life and vibrates with its own rhythms. And in this he finds a new source of happiness that can never dry up.

"I cannot tell you," Rousseau wrote to Malesherbes from Montmorency in 1762, "how much it has moved me that you think of me as the unhappiest of men. If only my fate were known to the whole world! If it were known, every one would want the same for himself; peace would reign on earth; men would seek no longer to injure one another. But what is it, then, that fills me with joy when I am alone with myself? I rejoice in myself, in the entire universe, in all that is and that can be, in all that is beautiful in the world of the senses, the world of the imagination, and the world of the mind.

"Which period of my life is it that I recall most gladly during my sleepless nights and to which I return most often in my dreams? Not the pleasures of my youth—they were too few, too mixed with bitterness, and they are too far behind me—but rather the periods I spent in retreat: my solitary walks, those ephemeral

[3] [Premier Dialogue (Hachette ed., IX, 144–45).]

86

but precious days I spent all by myself, with my good and unpretentious companion, with my dog and my cat, with the birds of the field and the animals of the woods, with the whole of nature and with its inconceivable Creator. As I rose before daybreak, in order to behold and enjoy the awakening of the sun in my garden, and when its rising promised a fine day, my first wish was that neither letters nor visitors should come to break the spell. I hastened away—and how my heart would beat, how I would breathe in overpowering joy when I felt certain that for the whole day I would be my own master! I would choose some wild spot in the forest, where nothing reminded me of the hand of man, where nothing spoke of man's tyranny, where no irksome third person could step between nature and myself. There an ever new magnificence would unfold before my eyes. The golden broom, the purple [heather] in which the world lay clad, enchanted my eye and stirred my heart. The majesty of the trees that covered me with their shade, the delicacy of the shrubs that surrounded me, the astonishing variety of flowers and herbs—all these would keep my mind in a continuous alternation of observation and wonder.

"My imagination would lose no time in populating this beautiful earth—and I filled it with beings after my heart's desire. Discarding all conventions and prejudices, all vain and artificial passions, I would cause to be born in the lap of nature and under her protection men who were worthy of living in her. In my imagination, I would create a Golden Age, and I was moved to tears as I thought of the true joys of humanity, of those delightful and pure joys which now are so far removed from men. Yet in the midst of all this, I confess, I felt at times a sudden sadness. Even if all my dreams had become reality, they would not have satisfied me. I still should have pursued my fancies, dreams, and desires. I would find in myself an inexplicable emptiness that nothing could fill—a striving of the heart for another kind of bliss, of which I could form no conception but which I yearned for nonetheless. And even in this longing there was pleasure, for I was filled in all my being with an acute emotion, with a sadness that attracted me and that I would not have wished to have taken from me." [4]

I have reproduced this passage from a letter at such length because it characterizes, with rare clarity and penetration, the new epoch which Rousseau was opening in the history of the European spirit. From here on the way lay open to the era of "sensibility" (*Empfindsamkeit*), of *Sturm und Drang,* of German and French romanticism.[5] Today, the *Nouvelle Héloïse* as a whole is remote from us; we cannot feel the immediate impact of the force with which it moved and shook Rousseau's century.[6] Its purely artistic

[4] Troisième Lettre à Malesherbes, 26 janvier 1762 [Hachette ed., X, 304–6]. [This passage, unlike other quotations, has been translated from Cassirer's German rather than from the original French, which Cassirer in his translation rearranged somewhat for the purpose of brevity. Despite numerous omissions and transpositions, Rousseau's meaning is not essentially changed, but in two passages Cassirer has treated the text rather freely. The passage, "As I rose . . . my own master," reads as follows in the Hachette edition: "En me levant avant le soleil pour aller voir, contempler son lever dans mon jardin; quand je voyais commencer une belle journée, mon premier souhait était que ni lettres, ni visites, n'en vinssent troubler le charme. Après avoir donné la matinée à divers soins que je remplissais tous avec plaisir, parce que je pouvais les remettre à un autre temps, je me hâtais de dîner pour échapper aux importuns, et me ménager un plus long après-midi. Avant une heure, même les jours les plus ardents, je partais par le grand soleil avec le fidèle Achate, pressant le pas dans la crainte que quelqu'un ne vînt s'emparer de moi avant que j'eusse pu m'esquiver; mais quand une fois j'avais pu doubler un certain coin, avec quel battement de cœur, avec quel pétillement de joie je commençais à respirer en me sentant sauvé, en me disant: 'Me voilà maître de moi pour le reste de ce jour!' " The passage translated as, "Yet in the midst of all this, I confess, I felt at times a sudden sadness," reads: "Cependant au milieu de tout cela, je l'avoue, le néant de mes chimères venait quelquefois la contrister tout à coup"—where "la" refers to "mon âme."]

[5] Cf. Erich Schmidt, *Richardson, Rousseau und Goethe* (Jena, 1875), for the literary influence and development of this theme.

[6] Rousseau offered characteristic examples of the influence of this work on his contemporaries in the *Confessions,* Livre XI. Cf. esp. the comprehensive Intro-

weaknesses now lie clearly before our eyes. Again and again, pure description and spontaneous expression of feeling are pushed into the background by the didactic tendency which guides this work from the start. In the end this tendency becomes so strong that it completely smothers the work of art; the second part of the novel bears an almost exclusively moralistic and didactic stamp. Even in the first part the tension between the two fundamental motives from which the work springs is unmistakable. We can hear the tone of abstract didacticism in the midst of the most glowing and most truthful description of passion. Occasionally the poetic style lapses suddenly into the style of the sermon; not infrequently Julie describes herself in her letters to Saint-Preux as a moral preacher—*la prêcheuse*.[7]

And yet, all this cannot repress the elemental force of the new feeling that here forces its way through. In individual pictures and scenes of the novel we immediately perceive the breath of a new era—as in that farewell scene in which Saint-Preux, compelled to leave his mistress and seized by the presentiment of eternal separation, sinks down in tears on the stairs which he has just descended and covers the cold stone with kisses. Here a new figure is born in literature: Goethe's Werther rises before us.

Yet Rousseau was not the first to mark the turn to "sensibility" in eighteenth-century literature. Richardson's first work, *Pamela,* had appeared in 1740, two decades before the *Nouvelle Héloïse,* and Richardson's novels awakened as much enthusiasm in France as in England. No less a man than Diderot became their champion and apostle. In his essay on Richardson he declares that if need should ever force him to sell his library he would keep, of all his books, besides the Bible, Homer, Euripides, and Sophocles,

---

duction to the critical edition of the *Nouvelle Héloïse* by D[aniel] Mornet ("Les Grands Ecrivains Français") [Paris: Hachette, 1925].

[7] *Nouvelle Héloïse,* Première Partie, Lettre 43 and elsewhere.

only the works of Richardson.[8] Thus "sentimentality" (*Sentimentalität*) as a purely literary phenomenon had long been familiar to eighteenth-century France. If, nevertheless, Rousseau was given up forever by the leaders of the intellectual movement of the century, after they had for a short time believed that they could draw him into their circle; if he appeared to them strange and incomprehensible, the reason for this may be found in the fact that he not only represented the elemental power of feeling but that he embodied it with unprecedented impressiveness. He did not describe this power: it was his very being and his life. And it was this life from which the spirit of the eighteenth century tried to protect itself, and which it tried to keep at a distance.

D'Alembert, who possessed not only intellectual genius but also a noble and refined soul, visibly attempted to do justice to his old adversary in his judgment on Rousseau's *Emile.* He conceded to him great literary gifts and a personal passion which only a few authors had ever possessed. "But Rousseau's passion," he adds, "seems to me to be of a more sensual than spiritual nature." "Malgré tout l'effet qu'elle produit sur moi elle ne fait que m'agiter. . . . Je ne prétends pas donner ici mon avis pour règle, d'autres peuvent être affectés différemment, mais c'est ainsi que je le suis." [9] That is an interesting and brilliant judgment, but it is not historically just. What D'Alembert perceived in Rousseau was the impetuous power of a "temperament" which he—in his sobriety and moderation, his prudence and superiority—felt to be hostile to his own nature. He resisted that power; he feared that by touching it he might lose the order and clarity, the methodical

[8] Cf. Diderot's essay on Richardson (*Œuvres,* éd. Assézat, V, 212ff.)

[9] D'Alembert, *Œuvres* (Paris: Didier, 1863), p. 295. ["In spite of all the impression which it makes on me it only disturbs me. . . . I do not mean to offer my opinion as the general rule; others might be affected differently, but that is how I am affected."]

safety of his spiritual world and be tossed back into the chaos of sensuality.

At this point Diderot, too, found the boundary of his otherwise almost unlimited gift for sympathy. His intuitive understanding of men and his faculty for enthusiastic devotion to friendship ultimately failed with Rousseau. He regarded Rousseau's untamable urge for solitude merely as a singular quirk. For Diderot needed sociable intercourse not only as the essential medium for his activity but also as the spiritual fluid in which alone he was capable of thinking. The will to solitude accordingly appeared to him as nothing less than spiritual and moral aberration. It is well known that Diderot's phrase in the postscript to the *Fils naturel,* that only an evil man loves solitude—a phrase that Rousseau immediately applied to himself and for which he took Diderot to task—gave the first impetus to their break.[10] After this break, Diderot's feeling of something uncanny in Rousseau's nature rose until it became almost intolerable. "[He] makes me uneasy," Diderot wrote on the evening of their last meeting, "and I feel as if a damned soul stood beside me. [. . .] I never want to see that man again; he could make me believe in devils and Hell." [11]

Such was the impression Rousseau made on the spiritual leaders of the French Enlightenment. They saw a *daemonic* force at work; a man possessed, driven about restlessly, whose tortured restlessness threatened to rob them of their intellectual property, on which they had believed themselves planted securely and firmly. To be sure, Rousseau's irritability and sensitivity, his melancholia and his morbid suspicions helped to accelerate the break with the Encyclopedists and to make it irreparable once it

[10] On this point cf. *Confessions,* Livre IX [Hachette ed., VIII, 326–27].

[11] Diderot's letter of December 1757 [to Grimm], in *Œuvres* [éd. Assézat], XIX, 446. [The letter in the Assézat edition is dated "October or November, 1757."]

had occurred. But the deeper cause of the antagonism lay else-where. A spiritual destiny was at work here which had to fulfill itself without the help of any individual. With Rousseau the spiritual center of the epoch was shifted, and everything that had given it inner security and firmness was negated. He did not re-form its results; he attacked its spiritual roots. The resistance against him was therefore historically justifiable and necessary: the conspiracy which Rousseau imagined was being hatched against him was in reality a reaction which had its origin and justification in the innermost instinct of spiritual self-preservation of the epoch.

On the other hand, it is true, we will not do justice to the depth of the antagonism that prevailed if we regard Rousseau merely as the prophet who held up the new gospel of "feeling," against the rationalist culture of the eighteenth century. Understood in this vague sense, "feeling" becomes a mere slogan in no way adequate to characterize the uniqueness, the true originality, of Rousseau's philosophical formulation of the problem. This formulation be-gins to take shape only when, not content with surrendering to the new power that inspires him and drives him forward, he inquires into the cause and justification of that power. And Rousseau by no means affirmed this justification without restrictions. He had become aware of the power of feeling too early and too profoundly to be able to surrender to it without resistance. Therefore, at the very point at which he described this power most rapturously, he set up against it another power, whose justification and necessity he defended no less enthusiastically. To this other power he en-trusted the task of guiding life and creating its inner shape. When Julie, in the *Nouvelle Héloïse,* wrests from herself in deepest despair the decision to renounce her lover forever, she directs a prayer to God in which she entreats him not to let her falter in her resolve: "Je veux [. . .] le bien que tu veux, et dont toi seul es la source. . . . Je veux tout ce qui se rapporte à l'ordre de la nature que tu as établi, et aux règles de la raison que je tiens de toi. Je remets mon cœur sous ta garde et mes désirs en ta main. Rends toutes mes actions conformes à ma volonté constante, qui est la tienne; et ne permets plus que l'erreur d'un moment l'emporte sur le choix de toute ma vie." [12]

At this point the order of "nature" is equated with the order of Providence and the order of reason, and it is viewed as a constant unshakable norm which must not be sacrificed to the uncertain and fleeting impulses of feeling. The firmness, the inner security and completeness of the will is invoked against the power of passion. And this antithesis is not merely one of the elements in the construction of the *Nouvelle Héloïse;* it is, rather, the idea on which the whole conception of the work primarily rests. For even the *Nouvelle Héloïse,* in which Rousseau allowed his sensual ardor and passion to flow more freely than in any other of his works, was by no means intended as an apotheosis of sensuality. The love which the book portrays for us is of different character and origin. Genuine love, the kind of love that takes hold of and fills the whole man, does not strive for mere gratification but for perfection: "Ôtez l'idée de la perfection, vous ôtez l'enthousiasme; ôtez l'estime, et l'amour n'est plus rien." [13] In the *Nouvelle Héloïse* Rousseau did not oppose this ethical ideal of perfection to the ideal of love; for him both were intimately and essentially

[12] *Nouvelle Héloïse,* Troisième Partie, Lettre 18 [Hachette ed., IV, 247]. ["I desire . . . the same good that Thou desirest, and of which Thou alone art the source. . . . I desire everything that conforms to the order of nature which Thou hast established, and to the rules of reason which I have from Thee. I place my heart under Thy protection and my wishes into Thy hand, Make all my actions consistent with my real will, which is Thine, and permit no longer that the error of a moment should undo the choice of my life."]

[13] *Nouvelle Héloïse,* Première Partie, Lettre 24 [Hachette ed., IV, 56]. ["Take away the idea of perfection, and you take away enthusiasm; take away esteem, and love is no longer worth anything."]

93

intertwined. If we feel, both in the style and content of the *Nouvelle Héloïse,* a great disparity—indeed a break—between the first and second part of the work, we must realize that Rousseau himself was not aware of such a break. For even as an artist he never renounced his ethical ideals and demands; he always reiterated the exalted nature of virtue and maintained it against all the assaults of feeling. It is only in this manner that Rousseau's "sentimentality" gains its specific character, and the power and extent of its historical influence become fully comprehensible only in this context.

By virtue of its original dual nature, this "sentimentality" could affect and fascinate minds of radically different stamps and could bring under its spell even those thinkers who kept themselves completely free of any kind of mere "sensibility." Here we may add the example of Lessing to that of Kant. In Germany, Lessing was the first to recognize Rousseau's significance. Immediately after the appearance of Rousseau's reply to the prize question of the Academy of Dijon he wrote an extensive critical review. "I cannot say," he wrote, "how much respect one feels for a man who speaks for virtue against all current prejudices—even when he goes too far." [14]

This admiration and appreciation comes to light even more clearly in Lessing's review of Rousseau's second philosophical essay, the *Discours sur l'origine et les fondements de l'inégalité.* "Everywhere Rousseau is still the daring philosopher who disregards all prejudices, no matter how widely they are accepted. He goes straightway to the truth, unconcerned with the sham truths which he must relinquish every step of the way. His heart has taken part in all his speculative meditations; consequently, he speaks with a tone completely different from that of a venal sophist whom selfishness or boastfulness have made into a

[14] Lessing, *Werke* (Lachmann-Muncker), IV, 394. (April, 1751.)

teacher of wisdom." [15] The immediate effect of Rousseau's writings, particularly in Germany, did not stem from Rousseau's proclamation of a new nature-feeling but rested primarily on the ethical ideals and demands which he advocated. Rousseau became the awakener of conscience before he became the awakener of a new nature-feeling. The renewal which he initiated was understood above all as an inner transformation, a reformation of outlook.

To be sure, if we wish to comprehend the heart of Rousseau's ethics, we must strictly observe the boundaries between systematic and psychological considerations. As soon as these boundaries are blotted out, a thoroughly unfocused and blurred picture emerges. Rousseau was acutely aware of his inability—which he lamented bitterly—to bring his life and his doctrine into true harmony. He believed that he could realize his fundamental demands by withdrawing from the corruption that stemmed from society, in which he saw the root of all evil—by resolutely rejecting all the demands of convention and by casting aside all merely conventional morality.

But a truly inner liberation could not be gained in this way. He lost himself more and more in fruitless, purely superficial opposition. He estranged himself from the world and in exchange gained nothing but a mere eccentric's existence, which drove him completely into himself and put him at the mercy of his morbid fantasies without possibility of salvation. Thus, in his own existence, rebellion against society led not to liberation but to self-destruction.

But it is completely mistaken to make Rousseau's ethics responsible for the weaknesses of his character and for the conduct of his personal life. Thus, for example, Karl Rosenkranz declares in his biography of Diderot that Rousseau's ethics is nothing but a "vague morality of the good heart. Such morality is, indeed,

[15] *Ibid.*, VII, 38. (July, 1755).

very popular, but it is even worse than the morality of the *intérêt bien entendu,* because it is even more casual and vague. It is the morality of the natural man who has not raised himself to the objective truth of self-determination through obedience to the moral law. In its subjective capriciousness it does both good and, occasionally, evil; but it tends to represent the evil as a good because the evil supposedly has its origin in the feeling of the good heart. . . . To do his duty in obedience to any kind of categorical command was intolerable to Rousseau. . . . So long as duty pleased him, he fulfilled it—but to obey duty for duty's sake he found unendurable." Rosenkranz does not exempt even Rousseau's politics from this verdict: indeed, he claims that Rousseau's basic political tendency is to assert the "sovereignty of every individual." [16]

It is hardly possible to think of a more drastic misunderstanding and distortion of Rousseau's ethical and political thought than that contained in this description. Every single line of this picture is drawn incorrectly. Far from wishing to create room in his social and political ideal for individual license, Rousseau in fact considered it the sin against the very spirit of all human community. Before the will, as general will, license makes a halt; confronted with the right of the whole, it relinquishes its every claim. At this point special interest must be silent. More: every merely subjective inclination, every insistence on individual feeling ceases.

Rousseau's ethics is not an ethics of feeling but the most categorical form of a pure ethics of obligation (*Gesetzes-Ethik*) that was established before Kant. In the first draft of the *Contrat social* [17] the law is called the most exalted of all human institutions. It is truly a gift of Heaven, by means of which man has

[16] K[arl] Rosenkranz, *Diderot's Leben und Werke* (Leipzig, 1866), II, 75. [The reference to the "sovereignty of every individual" is actually on p. 76.]

[17] On this draft cf. [Albert] Schinz, *La Pensée de J.-J. Rousseau*, pp. 354ff.

learned to imitate in his earthly existence the inviolable command-ments of the Deity. Nevertheless, the revelation which takes place in him is not transcendent but purely immanent. This form of voluntary obedience must not be subjected to any qualifications or limitations. Where mere power rules, where an individual or a group of individuals governs and forces commands on the com-munity, it is essential and reasonable to set limits to the ruler and to tie him to a written constitution which he may neither exceed nor alter. For all authority, by its very nature, is open to abuse, and its improper use must, if possible, be checked and prevented. True, all preventive measures remain fundamentally ineffective, for where the *will* to lawfulness as such is absent, even the most care-fully contrived "fundamental laws" that are put before the sover-eign as binding and inviolable cannot prevent his interpreting them in his own way and his applying them as he pleases. Simply to limit the quantity of power is futile if its quality—its origin and legitimation—is not changed. Against usurped authority all limi-tation is impotent; and all authority is usurped which does not rest on the free subordination of all to a universally binding law. Such limitation might possibly impose certain curbs on the exer-cise of arbitrariness, but it cannot erase the principle of arbitrari-ness as such.

On the other hand, where a truly legitimate constitution rules—that is, where law and law alone is recognized as sovereign—a limitation on sovereignty is self-contradictory. For here the ques-tion of quantity, of the mere extent of power, loses its significance; only its content matters, and this content admits of no "more" or "less." The law as such possesses not limited but absolute power; it commands and demands unconditionally. It is this spirit which underlies the design of the *Contrat social* and shapes its every de-tail.

Rosenkranz further accuses Rousseau of reacting against the

family as the foundation of the state and of regarding the political community as a mere aggregate of "atomistic persons." This reproach, too, does not hold true without qualifications.[18] It is true that Rousseau rejected the derivation of the state from the family—the purely patriarchal theory of the state. All too clearly he saw the danger of absolutism in the use to which this theory of the state had been put. In his *Patriarcha,* Robert Filmer had used the thesis that all human domination originally rested on paternal authority to prove the divine and unfettered right of kings—and in this matter Bossuet had stood at his side. Against such an exaggeration of paternal authority Rousseau claimed that it contradicted the principle of freedom, purely as a rational principle: for reason, as soon as it has awakened in man, must not be subjected to any kind of tutelage. Its legal coming of age, its self-determination is the very essence of reason and forms its inalienable fundamental right.[19]

But while Rousseau objected to deriving the authority of the will of the state from the fact of the family, he was far from holding the family in low esteem or from regarding it as socially insignificant. Rather, he expressly worked against its decomposition and destruction. In opposition to the mores of his time he became the eloquent advocate of the family and of the original ethical forces which he saw embodied in it. The entire second part of the *Nouvelle Héloïse* is devoted to this apologia of the family as a preserver and guardian of all human virtues. It is true, nevertheless, that this idealization of the family is subject to a qualification which we should least seek and suspect if we have merely the traditional version of his doctrine in mind. For while Rousseau

[18] [Cf.] Rosenkranz, *op. cit.,* II, 76.

[19] On Rousseau's opposition to the "patriarchal" theory of the state, cf. especially *Discours sur l'inégalité,* Seconde Partie (*Œuvres,* Zweibrücken [Deux-Ponts], 1782, pp. 129ff.) [Hachette ed., I, 118ff.], and the article "Economie politique" in the *Encyclopédie* [Hachette ed., III, 278-305].

revered and glorified the family as the natural form of the human community, he did not by any means regard it as the properly *ethical* form of this community. On the contrary, at this point all standards of measurement seem to shift suddenly; here the principles of judgment and valuation seem to turn into their opposites. Against mere feeling, Rousseau affirmed the primacy of reason; against the omnipotence of nature, he appealed to the idea of freedom. He did not wish to abandon the highest form of the human community to the naked domination of natural forces and instincts; rather, this form was to grow out of the force, and to exist in accordance with the demands, of the ethical will. We have now reached a decisive turning point. From here we can survey for the first time the complete development of Rousseau's thought, tracing his doctrine back to its first motives or following it forward in the direction of its ultimate aims.

If we apply traditional standards to Rousseau's doctrine and to its position in the philosophy of the eighteenth century; if we start from the premise that Rousseau's essential achievement lies in setting the cult of feeling against a limited and one-sided rationalist culture, we are placed before a strange anomaly in regard to the foundations and development of his ethics. Here if anywhere, Rousseau's supposed thesis would have to find its proper support and to stand its test. Is there any sphere of spiritual being in which the power of feeling could show and prove itself more strongly than in the sphere of morality? When has feeling a better right to rule and to guide than in the matter of establishing an immediate relationship of man to man? And yet, if we approach Rousseau's ethics and social theory with such expectations, we shall soon be disappointed.

For now the remarkable fact becomes apparent: Rousseau—in opposition to the predominant opinion of the century—eliminated feeling from the foundation of ethics. All ethical thought of the eighteenth century showed, despite deviations in detail, a common direction insofar as it understood the quest for the origin of morality as a psychological problem and as it believed that this problem could be solved only by penetrating the nature of moral feeling. This, it would seem, must be the point of origin and the pivot of every ethical theory. The point was made again and again that such a theory could not be devised arbitrarily and constructed from mere concepts but must rest on an ultimate unanalyzable fact of human nature. This fact was thought to have been discovered in the existence and peculiarity of the "feelings of sympathy." The philosophical ethics of Shaftesbury and Hutcheson, Hume and Adam Smith, were built upon the doctrine of the feelings of sympathy, the doctrine of the "moral sentiment."

The thinkers of the Encyclopedist circle also took this direction from the start. Diderot began his career as a philosophical writer with a translation of and commentary on Shaftesbury's *Inquiry concerning Virtue and Merit* and continued to cling unswervingly to the derivation of morality from the feeling of sympathy. This he regarded as an original psychological force *sui generis* which it would be futile to derive from mere self-love. When Helvétius attempted such a derivation in his book *De l'esprit,* denying any independent source to ethics and trying to prove vanity and self-interest the springs of all ostensibly ethical actions, Diderot explicitly opposed him.[20] He was certain that there could be only one trustworthy, or indeed possible, way of explaining the origin of the human community, and that was to prove that this community was no mere artificial product, but that it was rooted in an original instinct of human nature. The social contract did not create the community but merely gave form and external expression to a community that already existed.

This is the thesis which Diderot set forth and substantiated

[20] Cf. Diderot's criticism of Helvétius, in *Œuvres,* éd. Assézat, IX, 267ff.

thoroughly in the articles "Droit naturel" [21] and "Société" in the *Encyclopédie*, and it is precisely against this thesis that Rousseau directed his sharpest critical objections. He explicitly rejected the derivation of society from a "social instinct" that is part of man's original equipment. On this point he did not hesitate to go back to Hobbes in order to oppose the natural-law conception such as it had been founded by Grotius and further developed by Pufendorf. According to Rousseau, Hobbes had quite rightly recognized that in the pure state of nature there was no bond of sympathy binding the single individuals to each other. In that state everyone is on his own and seeks only that which is necessary for the preservation of his own life. According to Rousseau, the only flaw in Hobbes's psychology consisted in its putting an active egoism in the place of the purely passive egoism which prevails in the state of nature. The instincts of spoliation and violent domination are alien to natural man as such; they can come into being and strike roots only after man has entered into society and has come to know all the "artificial" appetites it fosters. Accordingly, the striking element in the mentality of natural man is not violent oppression of others but indifference and unconcern toward them.

It is true that according to Rousseau even natural man is capable of compassion; but this very compassion is not rooted in some originally "ethical" quality of man's will but merely in man's gift of imagination. Man has the inborn ability to enter into the being and sentiments of others, and to a certain extent this capacity for sympathy permits him to feel the sufferings of others as his own.[22]

[21] That the article "Droit Naturel" in the *Encyclopédie* is by Diderot and not, as frequently assumed, by Rousseau, and that Rousseau sharply criticizes this article in the so-called "Geneva Manuscript" [i. e., the first draft of the *Contrat social*] seems to me beyond doubt, after a comparison of the texts. In this question I am in agreement with the verdict and the line of proof offered by [René] Hubert in his *Rousseau et l'Encyclopédie* [Paris, 1928].

[22] On Rousseau's "psychology of the natural man" and his criticism of Hobbes, cf. esp. *Discours sur l'inégalité,* Première Partie [Hachette ed., I, 86].

But this ability, based on mere sense impression, is still a long way from taking an active interest in others and from effectively standing up for them.

We commit a strange *hysteron proteron,* we confound beginning and end, if we regard this interest as the origin of society. A form of sympathy which transcends mere egotism may be the goal of society, but it cannot be its point of departure. Nor do we escape from this difficulty—indeed, we increase it—if instead of appealing to the mere feeling of the individual we appeal to his reason, which teaches him that he cannot reach his own happiness without at the same time promoting the happiness of others. "The whole scheme of society," writes Diderot in the article "Société" in the *Encyclopédie,* "rests on this universal and simple principle: I want to be happy, but I live with men who want to be just as happy; let us therefore look for a means of securing our own happiness by securing theirs, or at least without doing them harm." [23]

But the man who would seek the origin of society in considerations of this kind falls, according to Rousseau, into still another curious error of substitution. He makes a "philosopher" out of the natural man; makes him reflect and argue on happiness and unhappiness, on good and evil. In the state of nature there can be no harmony between self-interest and common interest. Far from being identical, the interest of the individual and the interest of society are mutually exclusive. And so, in the beginnings of society, social laws are simply a yoke that everyone wants to impose on others without thinking of subjecting himself to it.[24]

Thus, in contrast to the uncritical enthusiasm with which Diderot praised the state of nature as a state of innocence and peace, of happiness and mutual good will, Rousseau painted a very

[23] [*Œuvres,* éd. Assézat, XVII, 133.]

[24] Cf. Rousseau's article "Economie politique" in the *Encyclopédie.*

sober picture. Diderot has Nature address her children in the following apostrophe:

" 'O you,' says she, 'who in obedience to the instinct I have implanted in you strive for happiness at every moment of your existence, do not resist my highest law! Work on your happiness, enjoy without fear, be happy! [. . .] In vain, superstitious men, do you seek your well-being beyond the bounds of the earth on which my hand has placed you. [. . .] Dare to liberate yourselves from the yoke of religion, my proud rival who disdains my rights. Renounce its gods who have violently usurped my power and subject yourselves once more to my laws. [. . .]

" 'Return to me, [. . .] to nature; I shall comfort you, I shall free you from all the fears that oppress you, from all the unrest that tortures you, [. . .] from all the hatred that separates you from mankind, which you should love. Restored to nature, to humanity, to yourselves, scatter flowers on the path of life.' " [25]

Over against this lyrical excess, Rousseau's description of primitive man and community seems thoroughly harsh and unsentimental. His description also has many mythical traits, but compared with the idyl envisioned by Diderot or Bernardin de Saint-Pierre it appears almost realistic. For Rousseau no longer yielded to the psychological illusions that were so dear to the whole eighteenth century and which it liked to conjure up again and again. He defended "primitive man" against Hobbes inasmuch as he attributed to him neither an instinctual greed for power and possessions nor an inclination for the violent oppression of others, but he nevertheless refused to grant him spontaneous good will and natural generosity. He denied the existence of any primary instinct in man that drives him to community and keeps

[25] [Diderot, Œuvres, éd. Assézat, IV, 110; from the last chapter of Holbach's Système de la nature. Diderot's editors hold that this chapter is almost certainly Diderot's work, but the matter is not fully settled.]

him within it—and with this denial he attacked the foundation on which Grotius, Shaftesbury, and the majority of the Encyclopedists [26] had built their theories of the origin of society and morality.

But it would seem that we are thus faced with a new dilemma, even as far as Rousseau's own theory is concerned. For when Rousseau renounced the psychological optimism of the eighteenth century, he seemed to pull the ground out from under his own feet. Was not this optimism the strongest, indeed the only support for his thesis of the original goodness of human nature? And did not this very doctrine stand in the center of his whole philosophy—was it not the focal point of his metaphysics, his philosophy of religion, his doctrine of education? Did not this renunciation of psychological optimism drive Rousseau back into the dogma of original sin, which he rejected and combated so passionately?

But it was precisely at this point that a new path opened up for Rousseau. What was distinctive and characteristic in him was the circumstance that he sought protection against this theological pessimism in a place where Shaftesbury and natural law had not looked for it. For him the goodness of man, which he affirmed and championed now as before, was not an original quality of feeling but a fundamental orientation and fundamental destiny of man's will. This goodness is grounded not in some instinctive inclination of sympathy but in man's capacity for self-determination. Its real proof lies, accordingly, not in the impulses of natural good will but in the recognition of an ethical law to which the individual will surrenders voluntarily. Man is "by nature good"— to the degree in which this nature is not absorbed in sensual instincts but lifts itself, spontaneously and without outside help,

[26] On the various forms of social theory developed by the Encyclopedists, see above all the detailed account by [René] Hubert, *Les Sciences sociales dans l'Encyclopédie* (Paris, 1923).

to the idea of freedom. For the specific gift that differentiates man from all other natural beings is the gift of perfectibility. He does not tarry in his original condition but strives beyond it; he is not content with the range and kind of existence which are the original gifts of nature nor does he stop until he has devised for himself a new form of existence that is his own.

However, by thus renouncing the guidance of nature, man has also given up its protection and all the benefits which it had originally conferred upon him. He sees himself exiled to an unending road and abandoned to all its perils. Rousseau, especially in his first essays, never tired of depicting these dangers. Perfectibility is the source of all man's insights as well as all his errors, of all his virtues as well as his vices. It seems to raise him above nature, but it makes him at the same time a tyrant over nature and a tyrant over himself.[27] And yet we cannot dispense with it, for the course of human nature cannot be stayed: "La nature humaine ne rétrograde pas."[28]

We cannot resist "progress" but, on the other hand, we must not simply surrender to it. We must guide it and, in full independence, designate its goal. In man's evolution up to now, perfectibility has entangled him in all the evils of society, it has led him into inequality and bondage. Yet it, and it alone, can also become his guide through the labyrinth into which he has strayed. It can and must clear his way to freedom once more. For freedom is not a gift put into man's cradle by benevolent nature. It exists only insofar as he acquires it for himself, and its possession is inseparable from this ever-renewed acquisition.[29] Consequently, Rousseau did not demand from the human community that it

[27] *Discours sur l'inégalité*, Première Partie [Hachette ed., I, 90. Cf. above, p. 78].

[28] Cf. above, p. 54.

[29] [Cf. Faust's lines in Goethe's *Faust*, Part Two, Act V:
Nur der verdient sich Freiheit wie das Leben,
Der täglich sie erobern muss.]

should increase man's happiness, well-being, and pleasure—nor did he expect these benefits to result from the establishment and consolidation of a future community—but that it should secure his freedom and thus restore him to his true destiny. Against the utilitarian political and social theories of the Encyclopedists he set, clearly and firmly, the pure ethos of law. And in this ethos he ultimately found the highest, indeed the only proof of the original goodness of human nature. Only when we consider this point and evaluate it correctly in the whole context of Rousseau's fundamental position, can the new principle for which he stood be seen correctly.

It now appears that even his appeal to "feeling" conceals two thoroughly different tendencies. From the original power of feeling Rousseau gained a new understanding of nature; with it he put himself into the center of its living presence. The mathematical-logical spirit of the seventeenth and eighteenth centuries had converted nature into a mere mechanism: Rousseau once again discovered the soul of nature. Against the formalism and schematic abstraction of the "nature-system," such as we find it in Holbach's *Système de la nature,* he opposed the quickening flow of his "nature-emotion." Through it he found the way back to the reality of nature, to the abundance of its forms and life. Man cannot understand this abundance of forms except by surrendering to it directly. Thus passivity, the repose in the infinite variety of impressions which nature unceasingly bestows upon us, becomes the source of true gratification and true understanding.

But a new and more difficult problem arises for man when communion with nature, in the solitude and detachment of his self, is no longer his sole pursuit; when he finds himself transplanted into the turmoil of the world of men—the social world. Rousseau himself had discovered that all individual wealth and intensity of feeling were impotent against that world, which threatened to shatter them. Thus Rousseau, the sentimental enthusiast, became the radical political thinker.

He himself describes this turning point in his autobiography with the greatest clarity. In the *Confessions* he writes that he had first been put on the path of political theory and had received the original impulse for the plan for his *Institutions politiques* by his recognition that in human existence everything was basically connected with politics, so that no people would ever be anything but what the nature of its laws and of its political institutions made it.[30] Against *this* nature, however, we cannot remain in mere passivity. We do not find it as given: we must produce it, we must actively shape it. And this shaping cannot be entrusted to mere feeling; it must spring from ethical insight and foresight. Rousseau made it quite plain that this insight, as well, does not arise from mere "understanding"; the form of pure reflection cannot contain it. Nor can the principles of ethical conduct and of genuine politics be excogitated, computed, or demonstrated by pure logic. They possess their own kind of "self-evidence" (*Unmittelbarkeit*); this self-evidence, however, is no longer that of feeling but that of reason. The true principles of morality are based neither on authority, be it divine or human, nor on the power of syllogistic proof. They are truths that cannot be comprehended in any but an intuitive way; but this very intuition is denied to no one, because it constitutes the fundamental power and the essence of man himself. To attain this "inborn" understanding we need not follow the laborious paths of abstract analysis, education, or learning. To comprehend it in all its clarity and immediately-persuasive certainty, we need only remove the hindrances that lie between us and it.

[30] Cf. *Confessions*, Livre IX (near the beginning). Cf. above, p. 65. [The *Institutions politiques* was the large work on politics which Rousseau had planned and of which the *Contrat social* was to form a part.]

Beside the self-evidence of feeling, then, there stands the self-evidence of ethical insight; but the two do not have the same origin. For one is a passive, the other an active power of the soul. In the case of self-evidence of feeling, our faculty of devotion is at work; it alone can unlock nature to us, and it allows us to blot out our own existence, so that we may live solely in and with nature. In the case of self-evidence of ethical insight, we are concerned with elevating and intensifying this existence of ours; for thus only may we survey the task of man in its true magnitude. This task remains insoluble for the individual as such; it can be accomplished only within the community and by means of its powers. According to Rousseau, these powers go beyond the compass of mere "nature." Having renounced the utilitarianism of the Encyclopedist theory of society, he also renounced its naturalism. He did not found the human community on mere instinctual life; he regarded neither the pleasure instinct nor the natural instinct of sympathy as a sufficient and adequate foundation. For him, the true and the only secure basis lay rather ·in the consciousness of freedom and in the idea of law, which is inseparably connected with this consciousness. However, they both spring not from the passivity of feeling, from mere susceptibility, but from the spontaneity of the will. Rousseau appealed to this spontaneity in order to demonstrate—as against the determinism and fatalism of the *Système de la nature*—that the self is underived and original, and that the sense of "being oneself" is inalienable and underivable. "No material being is active of itself, but I am active. There is no sense in arguing with me about this, I feel it, and that feeling which speaks to me is stronger than the reason which combats it. I have a body on which others act and which acts on them; this reciprocal action is beyond doubt; but my will is independent of my senses. [. . .] When I give myself up to temptations I act in accordance with the impetus given by external objects. When I reproach myself for this weakness, I listen only to my will. I am a slave through my vices, and free through my remorse; the feeling of my freedom is wiped out in me only when I become corrupted and when, in the end, I prevent the soul from raising its voice against the law of the body." [31]

Thus even the ethical conscience remained for Rousseau a kind of "instinct"—for it is not based simply upon reflective cogitation but springs from a spontaneous impulse. But a sharp line is nevertheless drawn between it and the purely physical instinct of self-preservation. Conscience is not merely a natural but a "divine" instinct: "Conscience! Conscience! instinct divin, immortelle et céleste voix, guide assuré d'un être ignorant et borné, intelligent et libre; juge infaillible du bien et du mal, qui rend l'homme semblable à Dieu. C'est toi qui fais l'excellence de sa nature et la moralité de ses actions: sans toi je ne sens rien en moi qui m'élève au-dessus des bêtes, que le triste privilège de m'égarer d'erreurs en erreurs à l'aide d'un entendement sans règle et d'une raison sans principe." [32]

It is only with these famous sentences from the "Profession de foi du vicaire savoyard" that we have reached the real center of Rousseau's doctrine of feeling. His specific originality is only now fully disclosed, and we glimpse the new dimension which sharply distinguishes it from the various tendencies of "sentimentality" of the eighteenth century. Rousseau's "sentimentality" was rooted in his nature-understanding and nature-emotion, but from these

[31] "Profession de foi du vicaire savoyard," in *Emile*, Livre IV [Hachette ed., II, 251].

[32] [*Ibid.* (Hachette ed., II, 262).] ["Conscience! Conscience! Divine instinct, immortal and celestial voice! Sure guide of a being ignorant and limited, yet intelligent and free! Infallible judge of good and evil, making men resemble God! From you comes the excellence of man's nature and the morality of his actions: without you, I feel nothing within myself that raises me above the beasts, except for the sorry privilege of straying from error to error, with the help of an intelligence without order and a reason without principle."]

roots it rose into a new world: it pointed the way into the "intelligible" and found its true fulfillment only in that realm. Thus feeling is, in the meaning which Rousseau gave it, a "citizen of two worlds."

A peculiar circumstance in Rousseau's use of language makes an understanding of this situation difficult and has again and again confused the historical judgment of Rousseau. Rousseau's terminology designates with a single expression the two fundamentally different dimensions into which feeling enters. The word *sentiment* bears now a purely naturalistic, now an idealistic stamp; it is sometimes used in the sense of mere sentiment (*Empfindung*), sometimes in the sense of judgment and ethical decision. One must pay careful attention to this double meaning, which, as a matter of fact, appears to have hardly ever been noticed by writers on Rousseau; for, if this double meaning is ignored, the tortuous threads of Rousseau's doctrine threaten to become tangled up again and again. At times, feeling (*sentiment*) is for Rousseau a mere psychological affect; at times, it is a characteristic and essential action of the soul. "I exist, and I have senses through which I am moved. That is the first truth that strikes me and in which I am forced to acquiesce. Have I a specific feeling of my existence (*un sentiment propre de mon existence*) or do I perceive it only through my sense perceptions (*ou ne la sens-je que par mes sensations*)? That is my first doubt, and at the moment I cannot solve it. Since I am continually moved by sense perceptions—either directly or through memory—how can I know if the feeling of *myself* is something beyond these same sense perceptions, and if it can exist independently of them." [33]

There are two ways out of this doubt. One way, that of deliberative judgment, leads us to an area of consciousness that cannot be comprehended by mere sentiment. In sentiment, con-

[33] [*Ibid*. (Hachette ed., II, 240). The French passages are in Cassirer's text.]

tents offer themselves to us singly as isolated units; in judgment, this isolation ceases. Different ideas are compared with each other, and relationships are established among different objects. It is this faculty of analysis and synthesis alone which gives the copula of judgment, the word "is," its characteristic significance. The objective meaning of this "is" cannot be comprehended by means of mere sentiment; nor can sentiment explain the logical power inherent in it. To understand this meaning and this power we must go back to a spiritual activity, not to a mere passive condition. "I seek in vain in a purely sensual being that intelligent force which compares and then judges; I cannot see it in its nature. This passive being will perceive each object separately [. . .] but, having no faculty for interweaving one object with another, it will never compare them, and it will not pass judgment on them. [. . .] Comparative ideas, such as *greater, smaller,* just as numerical ideas such as *one, two,* etc., are certainly not sense perceptions, although my mind produces them only when my sense perceptions occur." [34]

Even the phenomenon of error can be understood only on this basis. For error as such never rests on a simple deception of the senses but on a mistake in judgment. In the mere passive reception of an impression no deception takes place. Deception is produced only when the spirit acts on the impression, when it makes a decision concerning the reality or unreality, the being-so or not-being-so of the object which corresponds to the impression. And a new world opens up once again. For the proper sphere in which our self is again and again called upon to make such decisions is not theoretical but practical conduct. The very essence of the self, the fullness and depth of self-awareness, is, therefore, disclosed not in thought but in the will. Again, this feeling of self-awareness is most sharply distinguished by Rousseau from

[34] [*Ibid.* (Hachette ed., II, 241).]

mere "sensation" on the basis of its character as well as its origin. But on the other hand it must be equally clearly differentiated from mere logical operations, from the acts of thought and judgment. "Les actes de la conscience ne sont pas des jugements, *mais des sentiments;* quoique toutes nos idées nous viennent du dehors, *les sentiments qui les apprécient sont au dedans de nous,* et c'est par eux seuls que nous connaissons la convenance ou [la] disconvenance qui existe entre nous et les choses que nous devons rechercher ou fuir." [35] The circle of Rousseau's theory of feeling is completed only at this point: feeling is now raised far above passive "impression" and mere sense perception; it has taken into itself the pure activities of judging, evaluating, and taking a position. And only now has it achieved its central position in the constellation of psychological capacities. It no longer appears as a special faculty of the self but rather as its proper source—as the original power of the self, from which all other powers grow and from which they must continually take nourishment lest they wither and die.

Feeling is capable of achieving this result through its inherent dynamic momentum, which according to Rousseau constitutes its essential characteristic. The return to the dynamics of feeling discloses a deeply hidden layer of the self in which sensationalist psychology, keeping to the surface of mere impressions, is doomed to failure. Thus Rousseau returned, in a thoroughly individual way, from Condillac to Leibniz. Historically, this turning point is all the more remarkable since we can nowhere observe any direct influence that Leibniz's fundamental thought might have exercised on Rousseau. The epistemology which Rousseau wove into

[35] *Ibid.* [Hachette ed., II, 261]. ["Acts of consciousness are not judgments *but feelings.* Although all our ideas come from outside, *the feelings that appraise them are within us,* and it is through these feelings alone that we have knowledge of fitness or unfitness of the relationship between ourselves and the things that we must seek out or avoid." Italics added by Cassirer.]

the "Profession de foi du vicaire savoyard" frequently reminds us line by line of Leibniz's *Nouveaux Essais*—but it is known that this work was published only in the year 1765, from the manuscript in the Library in Hanover, three years after the appearance of *Emile*.

Still more significant than the renunciation of Condillac's philosophy is the motive from which this renunciation sprang. For a long time Rousseau had stood completely under the spell of Condillac's principles. He was not only Condillac's close personal friend; from his early years he had also considered him his admired guide and his master in all questions of epistemology and analytical psychology. Even in *Emile* this dependence had by no means been overcome. Throughout the book, it still stands out unmistakably in the manner in which Rousseau lets his pupil rise step by step from the "concrete" to the "abstract," from the "sensual" to the "intellectual." Essentially, we see here nothing but the pedagogic application of that famous figure which Condillac had coined in his *Traité des sensations*—the figure of the statue which is gradually awakened to life as the individual senses inscribe their impressions on it.

But by following this figure through consistently, Rousseau was led to the limits of its applicability. It may be true that all knowledge of external reality rests on nothing but an accumulation and combination of sense impressions: but the inner world can neither be explained nor constructed in this manner. We may breathe the life of sentiment into the dead marble, and we may allow this life to expand ever more, until at last the whole horizon of things, of visible objects, discloses itself to us in it. But what we do *not* give the statue in this fashion, what we cannot instill into it from the outside, is the feeling of spontaneity and the consciousness of the will that is rooted in that feeling. Here all analogies with external, mechanical happenings are bound to fail; the thread snaps

—that thread of association on which Condillac's doctrine would string all psychological contents and all psychological events. For activity cannot be explained by passivity any more than the unity of the self, the unity of the ego's ethical character, can be derived from the multiplicity of mere "sensations." As soon as we immerse ourselves in the nature of the will, as soon as we wish to understand its character and its fundamental law, we must accept the risk of stepping into a world other than the one which sense perception discloses to us.

At this point, therefore, Rousseau's break with all "positivism" became inevitable. He desired and accomplished this break not as an epistemologist but as a moralist. D'Alembert applied the methodological principle of positivism consistently in his *Eléments de philosophie,* even in laying the foundation of morality and of social philosophy. "Society," he declares, "has grown out of purely human needs and is founded on purely human motives. Religion has no share in its original formation. [. . .] The philosopher is satisfied with showing man his place in society and leading him to it; it is left to the missionary to drag him again to the foot of the altar." [36]

For Rousseau, however, the question could no longer be put in this way. In agreement with all the Encyclopedists, he too repudiated a transcendental justification of ethics and of political and social theory. Man cannot be relieved of the task of ordering his world; and in shaping and guiding it, he neither can nor ought to rely on help from above, on supernatural assistance. The task has been put to *him*—and he must solve it with his own, purely human means. But precisely as he penetrates into the character of the problem before him, he acquires the certainty that his self is not confined to the limits of the world of sense. From immanence

[36] D'Alembert, *Essai sur les éléments de philosophie,* [Chap.] vii, in *Mélanges de littérature, d'histoire et de philosophie* (nouv. éd.; Amsterdam, 1763), p. 80.

and from ethical autonomy, man now pushes forward into the core of "intelligible" being. By giving the law to himself he proves that he is not completely subject to the control of natural necessity.

Thus for Rousseau the idea of freedom was inextricably linked with the idea of religion—not in the sense that freedom is based upon religion, but in the sense that religion rests on freedom. Henceforth, the center of gravity of religion lies solely and simply in ethical theology. And this is the very trait which distinguishes Rousseau's philosophy of religion from all empiricist and positivist conceptions as well as from all forms of religious pragmatism. In his book on Rousseau, which attempts to give a new interpretation of his doctrine as a whole, Schinz has pushed the religious doctrine of Rousseau quite close to the modern forms of pragmatic religiousness. For Rousseau, Schinz claims, the meaning of religion amounts to nothing more than its efficacy; and its highest, indeed its only, achievement consists in its promoting and ensuring the happiness of man. Its truth remains dependent upon the fulfillment of this task. In the sphere of religion there is no pure abstract truth; only that is valid which has immediate reference to the concrete existence of man, which influences, upholds, and promotes it. Therefore, whatever neither points toward this aim nor directly serves it can have no lasting religious validity and certainty. Thus, according to Schinz's interpretation, it was far less important for Rousseau to found a "true" philosophy than it was to found a useful philosophy—and by the latter Rousseau understood a doctrine that secures to man his happiness not only in the life to come but already here on earth.[37] This interpretation undoubtedly characterizes a certain element in Rousseau's fundamental religious conception, but it by no means lays bare its real core. For this core is to be found not in the problem of happiness but in the problem of freedom.

[37] Schinz, *La Pensée de J.-J. Rousseau,* pp. 466, 506, and elsewhere.

Like the whole eighteenth century, Rousseau wrestled again and again with the problem of reconciling "happiness" and "virtue," of harmonizing "being happy" and "deserving to be happy." But it was precisely through these struggles that his inner self outgrew the eudaemonist statement of the problem. His tendency to assign to happiness itself a purely "intelligible" purpose instead of a purely sensual one became increasingly marked. Only that which leads man toward this purpose and which strengthens him in it can truly and essentially be called happiness. Thus it is not by allowing our instincts to flow freely but by restraining and mastering them that we can secure the highest happiness—the happiness of the free personality. Just like the epistemology and the ethics which Rousseau advocated in the "Profession de foi du vicaire savoyard," so the theory of religion centers at this point: all the threads of Rousseau's philosophy are gathered together in the idea of personality, not in that of happiness.

Furthermore, the development of Rousseau's philosophy of religion is also completely dominated by this thought. It emanates from the principle that when personality is to be given a *dos moi pou sto,* an assured and safe center, all merely peripheral considerations must be kept away. Here every form of mere mediation fails; for it is of the essence of mediation that its result will likewise possess only mediate value, that it can never gain conclusive and absolute significance. Religious certainty can never be anything but the certainty arrived at by the individual self—the acquisition of assurance through the self and for the self. It can never be a certainty acquired through external knowledge and testimony. Everything that is built on such inadequate foundations, everything that appeals for support to transmitted knowledge and to knowledge capable of being transmitted, loses by this very fact its religious value. Even if we could convince ourselves of the "objective" truth of such tradition, the very form of its proof would suffice to rob it of all religious content. The abundance of empirical and historical evidence cannot bring us closer to the real origin of religious certainty but draws us ever farther away from its original source. Only when man discovers the existence of God in his own existence—when, out of the direct knowledge of his own nature, he understands the nature and essence of God—only then will he gain the key to this certainty.

Whoever understands nature and religion differently transforms it into mere credulity in miracles or books—but through this very fact he demonstrates that he possesses a kind of certainty that he regards more highly than the true self-experience of the religious man. It is only distrust of this self-experience that makes men grasp for evidence and proof of a different sort. Yet whoever distrusts himself can depend upon others only by virtue of an inner contradiction. The significance of Rousseau's philosophy of religion for cultural history can therefore be described in a single phrase: he eliminated from the foundation of religion the doctrine of *fides implicita*. No one can believe for another and with the help of another; in religion, everyone must stand on his own and dare to wager his entire self. "Nul n'est excepté du premier devoir de l'homme; nul n'a droit de se fier au judgement d'autrui." [38]

There is no doubt that with these propositions Rousseau once more returned to the actual central principle of Protestantism; but this very return was a genuine discovery in view of the historical form of Protestantism in the eighteenth century. For neither Calvinism nor Lutheranism had ever radically overcome the

[38] ["Profession de foi du vicaire savoyard," in *Emile*, Livre IV (Hachette ed., II, 278).] ["No one is exempt from the first duty of man; no one has the right to rely on another's judgment." The Hachette edition has *exempt* instead of *excepté*.]

doctrine of the *fides implicita:* they had only shifted its center by replacing faith in tradition with faith in the Word of the Bible. But for Rousseau there existed no kind of inspiration outside the sphere of personal experience; for him the deepest, indeed the only form of self-experience was the experience of the conscience. All genuine and original religious knowledge flows from and subsists within the conscience—what cannot be derived from this source and is not fully contained and circumscribed in it is superfluous and questionable.

It was surely no accident that Rousseau did not reserve this profession of faith for a separate work but included it instead in *Emile.* This insertion is anything but a mere "literary" combination—it is founded in the general conception of *Emile.* This general conception can best be elucidated by viewing Rousseau's doctrine of education in the mirror of his doctrine of religion and, in turn, by viewing his doctrine of religion in the mirror of his doctrine of education. Indeed, both represent a single fundamental idea which they elaborate in different directions. The first part of *Emile* is intended to inculcate the maxim that even so-called external experience only *seems* to come to man "from outside." Even the circumference of the universe of the senses can be truly known only to the man who actually paces it off. The art of education cannot consist in saving the student the trouble of this pacing off, in giving him in advance a certain amount of information about the physical world in the shape of firmly established "sciences." Such mediation can engender within him nothing but uncertain and problematical information; all it can do is enrich his memory: it can neither give form to nor provide the basis of his knowledge.

Even in regard to objects of sense perception, genuine insight is acquired by everyone for himself. It is the pupil's business to create this insight within himself, not the educator's to plant it in him. He understands (*kennt*) the world only inasmuch as he acquires and conquers it step by step. And this conquest cannot result from mere abstract, inactive "knowing" (*Wissen*). The physical world reveals itself only to him who has learned from early life to measure himself by it. If we attempt to reduce its forces to theoretical formulas, they will be only incompletely comprehended; if we are to become truly familiar with them, we must experience and master them in practice. Rousseau wants to let the knowledge of the physical emerge from such direct intercourse with objects. In every field, direct acquaintance with things —which can be attained only through activity—should prepare for and lay the basis of the knowledge of them. Therefore, even physics cannot properly be "taught" but must be built up by the pupil himself in the progress of his own experience. He should know nothing but what he tests on himself; should hold nothing to be true but what he apprehends directly.

Precisely the same prerequisite demanded here for sense experience is applied to "spiritual" experience in the "Profession de foi du vicaire savoyard." Here, too, the axiom of unconditional "autopsy" is valid—and this axiom of seeing-for-yourself and finding-for-yourself gains ever greater importance as we now enter the proper sphere of consciousness of self—the realm of personality. The postulate of autopsy is transformed into the postulate of autonomy. All truly ethical and religious conviction must be based on it; all ethical instruction, all religious teaching, remains altogether ineffective and sterile unless it confines itself from the outset to the purpose of pointing the way to the goal of self-knowledge and self-understanding. Thus the reformulation of the idea of education requires—and makes possible—a transformation, a "reformation" of religion. When Lessing later saw the development of religion in the image of the *Education of Mankind,* he reached a synthesis which Rousseau had already prepared and which was a necessary consequence of Rousseau's philosophy.

But while the unity of conception in *Emile* thus becomes clear, the difficulties which this work presents are by no means eliminated. Rousseau himself regarded it as the true culmination of his thought and literary production; he repeatedly pointed out that only in this book the goal became visible toward which the various tendencies of his thought had striven and in which they were united.[39] And yet, at first glance it seems difficult, indeed impossible, to maintain this unity. All the writings of Rousseau abound in paradoxes, but among them *Emile* is possibly his most paradoxical. In no other work does he seem to surrender so completely to the bent of imagination and intellectual construction; nowhere else does he seem so completely to have lost all feeling for the "sober reality" of things. From the very outset, the work stands outside the conditions of social reality. It releases the pupil from every kind of relationship to human society; it places him, as it were, into a vacuum. The walls of this prison close in on him ever more confiningly. He is carefully kept from all contact with society and its forms of life; he is surrounded instead by a mere mirage, a kind of social phantasmagoria, which the educator artificially conjures up for him.

And the strange thing is and remains that all this painstakingly constructed system of social fictions is designed to serve no other purpose than that of the truth, to liberate the pupil from the unnaturalness of social conventions, and to lead him back to the simplicity and plainness of nature. But is it not the height of unnaturalness thus to hide the existing order of things from the

[39] Cf. esp. *Rousseau juge de Jean-Jacques,* Troisième Dialogue. In the *Confessions* (Livre XI), too, Rousseau describes *Emile* as the "best and most important" of his writings. [In the *Confessions* (Hachette ed., IX, 16), Rousseau calls *Emile* "mon dernier et meilleur ouvrage."]

child? And, furthermore, is this attempt not doomed to failure from the outset? As a matter of fact, the educator finds himself compelled at every step to tolerate in silence the reality which he had sought to remove carefully from the eyes of the pupil; not only that, but he must even call upon that reality in order to make it serve his purposes. At decisive turning points of spiritual and ethical development, such external aid is required and employed —we may recall, for example, the conversation between Emile and the gardener, which is designed to convey and to make comprehensible to Emile the first idea of property. Thus the fanatical love of truth, which was to guide this system of education, ends up by degenerating into a curiously complicated system of deceptions, of carefully calculated pedagogical tricks.

Another question must now be raised: What is the real *telos* of this education? For what ultimate goal is Emile to be educated? Rousseau never tired of impressing on us that this goal must be sought not outside the child but only within the child's self. But what is the "self" with which we are here concerned? Is the individual as such really supposed to remain confined in his sphere? Should he be tolerated with all his eccentricity and obstinacy and be confirmed in them? Is it the aim of education to maintain and foster all peculiarities of the self, all its vacillating appetites and moods? Has it no universal aim, no objective standard?

Indeed, Rousseau has not infrequently been charged with having removed all such standards. He has been reproached not only with having eliminated compulsion from education but also with having repudiated and abandoned the concept of duty. "This education," it has been said, "lacks what is perhaps the foundation of all education: the concept of duty. We are creating a man. The true definition of man is, however, that he is a being that can feel obligation. [. . .] This, then, must be the foundation of education, of *humanitas* [. . .] and that is precisely what we do not find in Rousseau." [40]

Were we to accept this interpretation, Rousseau's doctrine of education would not only stand condemned as a system but would also become historically and biographically incomprehensible. For were not all of Rousseau's political essays animated by the strongest enthusiasm for the law? Had not Rousseau defined the true goal of all political theory as the planning of a constitution which in and of itself would guarantee the most nearly perfect and unconditional rule of the law? Can he have betrayed this demand in *Emile?* Can he have put himself in flagrant contradiction with the *Contrat social,* which grants the individual will as such no room whatever but demands its unconditional surrender to, and identification with, the general will? Whoever expunges the concept of duty from the educational plan of *Emile* must indeed draw this conclusion; he must resort to the explanation that there is an irremovable and hardly comprehensible conflict between the pedagogy and the politics of Rousseau. Hence the same critic, faithful to this conception of Rousseau's doctrine of education, argues that Rousseau's political thought is a completely foreign body in the totality of his work—that the *Contrat social* stands in radical contradiction to all his other writings.[41]

But should we really assume that Rousseau's doctrine and personality are so radically split that they not only vacillate constantly between opposite extremes but even fail to become aware of the contradictions as such? It is difficult to adopt such canons of interpretation. Nor is it necessary to do so as long as an objective reconciliation between the tendency of *Emile* and that of the *Contrat social* is possible. And this reconciliation is not difficult

[40] [Emile] Faguet, *Dix-huitième siècle* (Paris, 1898), p. 356.
[41] *Ibid.,* pp. 383ff.

as soon as we understand that from the outset Rousseau used the word and the concept "society" in a double sense. He distinguished most sharply between the empirical and the ideal form of society —between what it *is* under present conditions and what it *can* and in future *ought* to be.

Rousseau's plan of education by no means rules out Emile's education to citizenship, but it educates him exclusively to be a "citizen among those who are to be." The society of his day was not ready for this plan. One should take care to keep that society at a distance, so that its empirical "reality" does not obscure the ideal possibilities which are to be established and to be upheld against the skepticism of the century. The power which holds contemporary society together is none other than that of convention, of habit, of natural inertia. This society will never change if it is not confronted with a categorical duty, an unconditional will to renewal. And how could such a will come into being, how could it be formed and strengthened, so long as the individual constantly moves in the sphere of society, becomes the slave of its morality and its habits, its preferences and its prejudices?

This spiritual and ethical decay the educational plan of *Emile* desires to prevent. It places the pupil outside society in order to protect him from infection and to let him find and go his *own* way. But this kind of individualism, this awakening to independence of judgment and will, by no means includes the will to isolation as a definite requirement. Just as Lessing's Nathan fears for Al-Hafi, so Rousseau fears for his pupil that he might "forget how to be a man merely by being among men." [42] Rousseau therefore excludes the cooperation of *societas* precisely for the sake of

[42] [See Lessing, *Nathan der Weise,* Act I, Scene 3:
    . . . Al-Hafi, mache, dass du bald
    In deine Wüste wieder kommst. Ich fürchte,
    Grad' unter Menschen möchtest du ein Mensch
    Zu sein verlernen.]

humanitas, for he separates most sharply the universal significance of humanity from its mere collective significance. He renounces the collectivity of men in order to found a new and truly universal humanity. This task does not require the collaboration of many— for every individual is capable of discovering within himself and by his own power the original pattern of humanity and of shaping that pattern out of his own self.

Rousseau categorically denies the educational power of example. Example polishes and levels, it stamps a common face upon all who follow it. But what everybody has in common is by no means the truly and genuinely universal. On the contrary, the universal can be discovered only when every man follows his own insight and recognizes, in and by virtue of this very insight, a necessary solidarity between his will and the general will. But this, to be sure, requires a long journey. The step which is required here cannot be taken during childhood. For that step is a prerogative, is indeed the distinctive mark and privilege of *reason* —and the child possesses reason only as a "talent" as yet incapable of effective action. Any attempt to force this talent into effective action prematurely would be futile. Rousseau unconditionally rejects all "moralizing" as such, all inculcating of abstract ethical truths, even when it takes a form which the child supposedly understands, as for example the fable.

Here, too, Rousseau advocates the ideal of "negative" education. The educator cannot speed up the evolution of reason; he can only ease its progress by removing the hindrances that stand in its way. When the educator has succeeded in checking these hindrances, he has done all he can ever do. All the rest ought to be exclusively the work of the pupil: for in the world of the will every one is truly only that which he has made of himself and by himself.

No matter what we may think of this fundamental Rousseauist conception as a system, one thing is certain: between it and the rest of Rousseau's work there is no discrepancy whatever. At this point, pedagogy and politics, ethics and religious philosophy fully interlock; they are but developments and applications of a single principle. And thus another contradiction is resolved. We have seen that Rousseau denies to men an original "social instinct" and refuses to base society on such an instinct. In *Emile* it would seem at first as if this doctrine, too, had been forgotten, for in the middle of the "Profession de foi du vicaire savoyard" we find once more the appeal to an original social inclination. From it Rousseau seemed to derive the concepts of duty and of conscience: "Quelle que soit la cause de notre être, elle a pourvu à notre conservation en nous donnant des sentiments convenables à notre nature. . . . Ces sentiments, quant à l'individu, sont l'amour de soi, la crainte de la douleur, l'horreur de la mort, le désir du bien être. Mais si, comme on n'en peut douter, l'homme est sociable par sa nature, ou du moins fait pour le devenir, il ne peut l'être que par d'autres sentiments innés, relatifs à son espèce; car à ne considérer que le besoin physique, il doit certainement disperser les hommes au lieu de les rapprocher. Or c'est du système moral formé par ce double rapport à soi-même et à ses semblables que naît l'impulsion de la conscience. Connaître le bien, ce n'est pas l'aimer: l'homme n'en a pas la connaissance innée; mais sitôt que sa raison le lui fait connaître, sa conscience le porte à l'aimer; c'est ce sentiment qui est inné." [43]

[43] [Hachette ed., II, 261–62.] ["Whatever the cause of our being may be, it has provided for our preservation in giving us feelings suited to our nature. . . . These feelings—as far as the individual is concerned—are self-love, fear of pain, dread of death, desire for well-being. But if, as is undoubtedly the case, man is sociable by nature, or at least capable of becoming sociable, he can be so only by means of other innate feelings relative to his species. For, considered by itself, mere physical need would certainly disperse men rather than bring them together. Now, it is out of the moral system constituted by that twofold relationship of man to himself and of man to his fellow men that the impulse of conscience is born. To know the good is not to love it: man has no innate knowledge of it. But as soon

But if, according to this passage, a necessary relationship with the community is inherent in the individual, if this relationship is in no way thrust upon him but is "inborn," does that not mean that we sin against nature if we deny its free unfolding? Do we not put a merely arbitrary product of art in place of the real man, creating an *homme de l'homme* and passing by the *homme de nature?* Once again it is necessary to avoid the ambiguities of Rousseau's concept of nature. The bond connecting man with the community is "natural"—but it belongs to his rational, not his physical, nature. It is reason which ties this bond and which, out of its own character, determines the nature of this bond. Thus even Rousseau considers man a political being—provided that man's nature be equated with his destiny—but not a political *animal,* not a *zoon politikon.* The biological justification of society is given up and is replaced by a purely ideal, an ethical justification. This ideality, however, cannot be expected of the child as such. The child's mode of living and his understanding do not reach beyond the sphere of instinctual life. And this limitation of his mode of living cannot be changed through mere teaching. We must therefore renounce all ethical exhortation and instruction, since it is condemned to impotence from the very start. Here, too, we must allow the pupil to find what he necessarily will and must find as soon as the time has come for him to participate in the "play of ideas." From this kind of ethical idealism, Rousseau was firmly convinced, there will grow a genuine, political-social idealism. Man will no longer regard the mere gratification of instincts as the goal of the community, nor will he judge the community by the degree to which it succeeds in securing such gratification. He will look upon it rather as the founder and guardian of the law—and he will understand that in the fulfillment of this task it secures, if not the

as his reason makes him know it, his conscience leads him to love it; it is this feeling that is innate."]

happiness, then certainly the dignity of man. This is the sense in which Kant read and interpreted Rousseau's *Emile:* and it may be said that this interpretation is the only one which preserves the inner unity of Rousseau's work and which fits *Emile* into the work as a whole without inner break and contradictions.

If we recapitulate the result of these considerations, it becomes apparent how long and difficult a path Rousseau had to travel before he succeeded in translating into purely intellectual form the basic personal experiences from which he started at every point and in representing them in the context of an objective philosophical doctrine. A strictly systematic elaboration and justification of this doctrine was not the goal for which he strove, nor did he feel equipped for it. "Systems of all sorts," he once wrote in a letter, "are over my head. . . . Reflecting, comparing, quibbling, persisting, [fighting]—these are not my business. I give myself to the impression of the moment without resistance and [even] without scruple; for I am perfectly sure that my heart loves only that which is good. All the evil I ever did in my life was the result of reflection; and the little good I have been able to do was the result of impulse." [44]

Not only the thought of Rousseau but also his style displays this peculiarity throughout. This style does not yield or submit to the strict standards which French classicism had set up as the fundamental laws of the *art de penser* and the *art d'écrire*. It persistently slips away from the strict line of argumentation: it is not content with letting the matter speak for itself but attempts to convey a completely personal, individual impression of that matter. There was nothing that Rousseau, as author, resisted as

[44] [From a draft of a letter to the elder Mirabeau, c. March 25, 1767, in *Correspondance générale de J.-J. Rousseau,* ed. Théophile Dufour (Paris: Colin, 1924–34), XVII, 2–3.]

vehemently as the ideal of an "abstract," coolly objective style. "When a lively conviction animates us, how should we then be able to speak in an icy language? When Archimedes ran naked through the streets of Syracuse in his excitement, was the truth which he had discovered the less true because it had filled him with such enthusiasm? To the contrary, whoever perceives the truth cannot help adoring it—the man who can remain cold toward it has never known it." [45]

Thus Rousseau remained, in his argumentation as in his language, "unique" and self-willed. He confessed this uniqueness proudly. "I am not made," he says at the beginning of his *Confessions,* "like any of those that I have seen; I dare believe that I am not made like anyone in existence. [. . .] Nature [. . .] has broken the mold in which she cast me." [46] And yet, no matter how strongly he remained aware of this uniqueness, Rousseau was animated by the strongest urge for communication and mutual understanding. He never renounced the idea of "objective" truth and the demands of an "objective" morality. Precisely for this reason, he made his intensely personal being and existence into an instrument of that idea. Unswervingly fixed and, as it were, submerged within himself, he nevertheless advanced to treating problems of absolutely universal significance—problems which even today have lost nothing of their force and intensity and which will long survive the accidental form, limited by his individuality and his time, that Rousseau gave them.

[45] *Lettres écrites de la montagne,* Avertissement [Hachette ed., III, 117].
[46] [*Confessions,* Livre 1 (Hachette ed., VIII, 1).]

ACKNOWLEDGMENTS

THE EDITOR acknowledges with gratitude the generosity shown by the following in making the publication of the Bicentennial Editions and Studies possible: the Trustees of Columbia University, the Trustees of Columbia University Press, Mrs. W. Murray Crane, Mr. James Grossman, Mr. Herman Wouk, and friends of the late Robert Pitney who wish to remain anonymous.

I want to thank, in addition, several colleagues and friends for their creative criticism of the Introduction. Professors Jacques Barzun, Richard Hofstadter, Franz Neumann, Henry Roberts, and Miss Gladys Susman read the drafts of my Introduction with a care and discernment for which I am grateful. Professors Ralph Bowen and Jack Stein helped me to track down several elusive citations, and Mr. J. Christopher Herold labored over both Introduction and translation far beyond an editor's call of duty.

Finally, I wish to acknowledge permission to quote several passages from C. E. Vaughan, *The Political Writings of Jean Jacques Rousseau* (Cambridge: Cambridge University Press, 1915), 2 vols.

P.G.